THE ART OF MYRRH BEARING

Encountering Christ
Through Serving Others

ELISSA BJELETICH DAVIS

ANCIENT FAITH PUBLISHING
CHESTERTON, INDIANA

Published by:
Ancient Faith Publishing
A Division of Ancient Faith Ministries
1050 Broadway, Suite 6
Chesterton, IN 46304

Unless otherwise noted, Scripture quotations are taken from the New King James Version, © 1979, 1980, 1982 by Thomas Nelson, Inc. Used by permission.

Quotations from the Book of Tobit are from the Orthodox Study Bible, © 2008 by St. Athanasius Academy of Orthodox Theology (published by Thomas Nelson, Inc., Nashville, Tennessee) and are used by permission.

Cover art and design: Amber Schley Iragui

ISBN: 978-1-955890-78-6

Library of Congress Control Number: 2025932565

Dedication

This book is written for my real-life myrrhbearers, especially Susanna and Ioanna, and for all the mothers—especially my mother, Susanne, and my mother-in-law, Martha. May we always be surrounded by myrrhbearers.

I offer this book with the prayer that my children, godchildren, and my husband and I all will find our way to truly embrace myrrhbearing as a way of life, in all its depth and beauty.

CONTENTS

Introduction   xi

Prologue: The Gospel's First Myrrhbearers   1

PART ONE
The Holy Myrrhbearers

Mary, the Mother of God   7

Mary Magdalene   17

Mary, the Wife of Clopas   23

Salome   29

Susanna   37

Joanna   41

Mary and Martha of Bethany   47

Nicodemus   55

Joseph of Arimathea   65

PART TWO
*Tracing the Myrrhbearers'
Journey in the Gospels*

Our Heavenly Myrrhbearer	71
The Unnamed Myrrhbearing Woman	75
The Women Disciples	81
The Hostess	87
Saved in Community	93
Waiting on the Lord	99
A Community Gathered	105
I Am the Resurrection	111
Jesus Wept	117
Lazarus, Come Forth!	121
To Bind and to Loose	125
Anointing for the Day of Burial	129
What Messiah Is This?	135
O Happy Tomb	141
Just Before Dawn	145
Resurrection	151
Go and Tell Your Brethren	157

PART THREE
Myrrhbearers in Action

Introduction	165
Tobit	167
Basil the Great	173

CONTENTS

John the Merciful   181

Cosmas and Damian   187

Righteous Joseph the Patriarch   195

Stylianos   205

John Maximovitch   211

Nicholas of Myra   217

Herman of Alaska   225

Olga of Alaska   235

Bishop Basil Rodzianko   247

Porphyrios of Kavsokalyvia   257

Mother Gavrilia   271

Maria Skobtsova (Mother Maria of Paris)   279

Afterword   289

Postscript: One More Myrrhbearer   295

Only if we truly give ourselves to Christ to labor with zeal, desire, and love for his body—only then will we find that that which we thought was impossible has been accomplished, that the stone which lies over each of our hearts, weighing us down, making us unable to see or feel God, that that stone will have been rolled away, and then we will no longer have merely a glimpse of what lies ahead, but be invited into the tomb, our heart, the bridal chamber.

Only God can remove the stone; but let us remember that we have to walk to the tomb! They had no idea how they were going to remove it; yet they went. So too must we walk to the tomb, prepared to roll away the stone without any clue about how we might do it, however futile we might think it to be to go to the tomb, weighed down by the heavy weight of our sin—the rock blocking our heart.

—Fr. John Behr[1]

---

1   Fr. John Behr, "The Sunday of the Holy Myrrhbearing Women," in *The Cross Stands While the World Turns: Homilies for the Cycles of the Year* (St. Vladimir's Seminary Press, 2014).

INTRODUCTION

What Is Myrrhbearing?

The Gospels tell us that when our Lord died, a quiet flurry of activity was set into motion. Joseph of Arimathea approached the authorities to request Jesus' body, and then he and Nicodemus quietly, gently brought Him down from the Cross. They had been powerless to stop the abuse and the crucifixion, but now they claimed His Body and were able to restore some measure of respect and dignity, wrapping Him in linens and spices and laying Him in a place of honor—in the new tomb Joseph thought he himself would lie in. They couldn't begin to understand what had happened here; they could not see the cosmic proportions of this event in salvation history that had taken place before their very eyes. They saw their Teacher, their Lord, defeated and killed, limp in their arms, and they did what they could to honor Him.

Each Gospel writer tells us, in his own way, that the women watched. Witnesses to every moment of His Crucifixion, they remained in place and saw where He was buried. They watched the Romans block the Tomb with a great stone and post guards to stand by, to prevent anyone from interfering with the end of Jesus Christ. They wanted to close this chapter and did what they could to prevent any further disruption from His small band of followers. The women observed the activity, and as the sun began to fade, signaling the Sabbath, obediently they went home to rest and waited for the hours to pass.

As the sun rose on that Sunday morning, the women were finally released from their Sabbath vigil; they waited exactly as long as God required and not a minute longer, emerging in the earliest moments of the day. They knew they weren't welcome at the Tomb, that both a tremendous stone and armed guards stood in their way. Without a plan, without any tool or weapon to force their way in, they simply showed up with arms full of myrrh and spices. One cannot guess how they hoped to gain access, but these women were not crushed, and they were not finished. Their stubborn love compelled them, and as the sun began to rise, they arrived, ready to prepare the body of their beloved Jesus.

For how many centuries had people brought myrrh to take care of their loved ones? The tradition goes back at least as far as ancient Egypt, a culture that perfected the art of honoring and preserving the human body. The Egyptians understood that myrrh is more than a sweet-smelling resin to cover the stench of death: It is both an antibacterial and a desiccant, actively fighting decay and corruption. For thousands of years, mourners brought expensive myrrh to wage one last battle against death, to offer one last burst of protest even as they buried the lifeless body of their beloved.

And indeed, on that morning, the women were showing up in protest; they refused to bury their love for Christ, and they refused to stop following Him. The authorities could beat Him, could kill Him, but these women would not be deterred. Armed with myrrh and spices, they arrived at the Tomb to prepare His body as one would honor a king; they came to the Tomb to proclaim the glory of our Lord.

Why would these women take such a risk? What is a dead body, that we should go to such pains to honor it? Christ's body had been respectfully and properly buried by Nicodemus and Joseph. There was no need to do more, so why would the women return to that Tomb on Sunday? What did myrrhbearing mean to them? Saint John Chrysostom offers insight:

> They had brought ointments, and were waiting at the tomb, so that if the madness of the Jews should relax, they might go and embrace the body. Do you see the women's courage? Do you see their affection? Do you see their noble spirit in money? Their noble spirit even unto death?
>
> Let us men imitate the women; let us not forsake Jesus in temptations. For they for Him even dead spent so much and exposed their lives, but we (for again I say the same things) neither feed Him when hungry, nor clothe Him when naked, but seeing Him begging, we pass Him by. . . . For indeed even now thou hearest Him say, You do it unto me; and there is no difference whether you give to this man or to Him; you have nothing less than these women that then fed Him, but even much more.[1]

The women went to Christ's Tomb to venerate His body, to serve Him even in death. They were courageous, affectionate, and noble. Saint John likens myrrhbearing, the caretaking of the dead body, with feeding the hungry and clothing the naked; he does not distinguish between serving a dead body and a living body. Indeed, myrrhbearing is nothing less than that very compassionate charitable activity to which Christ calls everyone who wishes to become His follower.

---

1   St. John Chrysostom, "Homily 88 on Matthew," trans. George Prevost and ed. M. B. Riddle, in *Nicene and Post-Nicene Fathers, First Series*, rev. ed., ed. Kevin Knight (New Advent), https://www.newadvent.org/fathers /200188.htm.

Why Become a Myrrhbearer?

Jesus does not ask for elaborate or dramatic action, but instead He calls us to love one another in profound and simple ways: We must feed the hungry, we must clothe the naked, we must visit the sick and the prisoners. In Matthew's Gospel, Jesus teaches that these essential, caretaking actions are the very basis for our final judgment at the end of days. For "when the Son of Man comes in His glory," He will say to those He judges worthy of the Kingdom of God,

> Come, you blessed of My Father, inherit the kingdom prepared for you from the foundation of the world: for I was hungry and you gave Me food; I was thirsty and you gave Me drink; I was a stranger and you took Me in; I *was* naked and you clothed Me; I was sick and you visited Me; I was in prison and you came to Me. (Matt. 25:34–36)

This real, concrete love is not a sidenote or a nice addition if you have time for it. Christ placed it front and center, positioning it as the defining factor in the Christian life: In the Last Judgment, this is the criteria He will use. The call to connect with and care for one another at the simplest, most basic level could not be more critical.

Many of us know certain Christians who live this calling more fully than others—they just seem to be built for nurturing and wired for thoughtfulness. As it happens, several of my friends who fit this bill happen to bear the names of the holy Myrrhbearers in the Gospels, so I have always associated their simple, merciful works of love—feeding, clothing, and visiting—with the work of the Myrrhbearers who lovingly prepared our Lord's body. Indeed, if we were to picture the perfect example of Christian caretaking— the good Samaritan who carefully poured oil and wine on the beaten man's wounds and then carefully wrapped him in bandages (Luke 10:33–35)—we might well envision a scene not unlike Joseph of Arimathea and Nicodemus lovingly pouring myrrh and aloes on our Lord's body, then wrapping Him in linens and laying Him down to rest.

The Importance of the Body

When God took on flesh in the Incarnation, He signaled the importance of the human body. On earth, Jesus ministered to bodies: He healed the sick and fed thousands with just a few loaves and fish. He taught us to follow His lead by physically caring for one another. He was crucified and rose again, showing us in His own resurrected body a glimpse of what our own bodies may look like after our resurrection: perfected and eternally alive. In the ultimate act of elevating the body, He ascended physically to the Father, bringing resurrected human flesh into heaven. And finally, He gives us His Body and Blood in the Eucharist.

The Church is more than a gathering of like-minded individuals; it is the Body of Christ: All our human souls and bodies join together in mystical communion, forming His Body. In his First Letter to the Corinthians, St. Paul famously describes the body as a temple: "Do you not know that your body is the temple of the Holy Spirit *who is* in you, whom you have from God, and you are not your own? For you were bought at a price; therefore glorify God in your body and in your spirit, which are God's" (1 Cor. 6:19–20).

We treat our own bodies as temples by refraining from sinful or polluting activity, but we must also treat each other's bodies as temples. As such, a gift of food to the hungry is an offering; indeed, what we give to the least of these is given to Christ, for we offer it to Him on the altar of our fellow man. Whether that person is dead or alive really does not matter, for death is overcome;

the temple of the Holy Spirit that breathes on earth will remain a temple even after its final breath.

We show our respect and love for one another by physically nourishing and nursing each other, but Christ calls us to something more than these actions: He asks us to visit the sick and the prisoners in their isolation, calling us to offer company and compassion to those in need of it. We aren't only to serve the body with food and drink; we are to enter into communion with one another. Surely when we break bread together, something more profound than feeding occurs. And indeed, when we gather to bury our beloved dead, we gather in community, consoling each other in our grief and drawing together in prayer. These activities are all manifestations of real love; their value transcends the practical service in these moments of communion, when our hearts reach out to connect with one another.

Myrrhbearing as a Metaphor

In this book I hope to share with you this expanded and deepened understanding of myrrhbearing as the fulfillment of Christ's commandment to love one another. Although the technical definition of myrrhbearing is to bring myrrh to prepare a body for burial, myrrh also can serve as a powerful metaphor: It is the healing, soothing oil of mercy, a sweet-smelling fragrance tinged with God's grace.

Oil often is understood by the Fathers to mean mercy and compassion. Take, for instance, how they understand the Parable of the Ten Virgins who awaited the Bridegroom in the middle of the night (Matt. 25:1–13). Jesus tells us that five of the virgins were wise, with plenty of oil for their lamps; five were foolish, with no oil on hand. Only the five wise virgins were ready when the bridegroom came, so only they were admitted to the wedding banquet. The Fathers read this allegorically: Christ the Bridegroom comes to take us to the banquet feast of heaven when we least expect Him. As Blessed Theophylact explains, "The lamps are our souls, and each one's mind is also a lamp; the lamp is lit when one has the oil of the virtues and of almsgiving." He continues, "But after God has given the light and a lamp, the wise, with their good deeds, add the oil."[2] Thus oil is virtue, almsgiving and good deeds.

All these women are virgins—that is, they live ascetically— but in addition to their purity, the virgins must have good works if they wish to enter the bridal chamber. Saint Gregory Palamas unpacks this idea in his sermon "On Christ's Second Coming":

> Not everyone who happens to be there is led into the bridecham- ber, only those adorned with virginity, which cannot be accom- plished without ascetic effort, self-control, and many different struggles in the cause of virtue. Besides they must hold lamps in their hands, which denotes their minds and the watchful knowl- edge enclosed within, borne up and supported by the practical part of their souls—as signified by their hands. Such knowledge must be dedicated to God for life and set alight with His bril- liance. But oil in abundance is needed to keep the lamps burning, and this oil is love, the summit of all virtues.[3]

Saint Gregory in no way demeans ascetic effort, but he does make it clear that all the fasting and prostrations in the world won't make up for a lack of this oil of love. If we wish to join Christ at the end of days, we will have to do all these things: We must fast

---

2 Bl. Theophylact, "On Matthew 25," in *The Explanation of the Holy Gospel According to St. Matthew*, Bl. Theophylact's Explanation of the New Tes- tament, vol. 1 (St. Herman of Alaska Brotherhood/Chrysostom Press, 1992).

3 St. Gregory Palamas, "Homily 4," in *The Homilies*, ed. Christopher Veni- amin (Mount Thabor Publishing, 2009), 29.

and study and pray, but we must crown all these efforts with loving service to others. The oil that allows us to enter the bridal chamber at Christ's Second Coming is love, shining forth in the good works to which He calls us. We must serve others not as mere duty, but as people who bear the sweet-smelling oil of love and compassion.

Ultimately, the goal of our Christian journey is to be transformed, to be filled with abundant new life; as St. John the Evangelist expresses it, "He must increase, but I *must* decrease" (John 3:30). If we hope to empty ourselves so that we may be infused with the Holy Spirit, we must first die to our own needs by loving and serving others. This is a long and mysterious process, but the good news is that we need take only the simplest steps: fast, pray, study, give alms. God will do much of the work, as long as we continue to show up and to love Him with all our hearts, minds, and souls, and love our neighbor.

In this book we'll explore the ways in which myrrhbearing can become a metaphor for the loving service that lies at the heart of our Christian life. We will find that being a myrrhbearer means being willing to serve, honor, and love our brothers and sisters, especially those who are broken and defeated. The love of the myrrhbearer takes on flesh—physical reality—and is evident in compassionate action. We will look to the examples of myrrhbearers in Scripture and beyond. If we can follow their lead to embrace this simple and profoundly beautiful way of life, we will grow as they did, into ever deepening communion with Christ and with others, whom He loves so very much.

Organization of This Book

In Part One we'll begin our consideration of myrrhbearing by getting to know the officially recognized Holy Myrrhbearers.

The Orthodox Church observes the official Sunday of the Holy Myrrhbearers on the third Sunday after Pascha, and identifies as Myrrhbearers those individuals who cared for Jesus' body after He was crucified: Joseph of Arimathea and Nicodemus; the Mother of God, Mary; Mary Magdalene; Mary, the wife of Clopas; Joanna, wife of Chuza, who was Herod's steward; Salome, the mother of the sons of Zebedee; Mary and Martha, the sisters of Lazarus; and Susanna.[4] They, along with the other women whose names we do not know, approached Jesus' Tomb early on Sunday morning to find angels declaring that He was not there, but had risen from the dead.

How to Use This Book

Each chapter is followed by questions for reflection. If you are reading this book in community, these questions might serve as jumping-off points for your discussion. If you are reading this on your own, take a moment to pause and consider the ideas they raise and where they may take you.

My great hope is that in the lives of our myrrhbearing brothers and sisters across the centuries, we will glimpse the great joy that lies at the heart of life in Christ.

Elissa Bjeletich Davis

---

4   See https://www.goarch.org/myrrhbearers-learn.

PROLOGUE

The Gospel's First Myrrhbearers

The first myrrhbearers to appear in the New Testament are not honoring a dead body, but quite the opposite: They arrive to celebrate a new life. This group of men left their homes and endured a long journey across desert lands to follow centuries-old prophecies in the hope of greeting a newborn king. This exotic band of visitors, "wise men from the East," tracked a star to Bethlehem, to the stable in which they found the infant Jesus. They entered the house, "saw the young Child with Mary His mother, and fell down and worshiped Him. And when they had opened their treasures, they presented gifts to Him: gold, frankincense, and myrrh" (Matt. 2:11).

These men—the first people to bear myrrh in the Gospels—are the magi, Babylon's star worshipers. Many years before, the faithful Prophet Daniel had been taken captive and taught Chaldean letters. He rose to prominence among the magi and wrote down sacred prophecies about the coming of a king. Centuries later—about fourteen generations—when, in God's time, the promise was fulfilled, the magi would follow a star to Bethlehem.

These magi were not among God's people; they were pagans. But God spoke to them in a language they could understand: He instructed them to watch the skies and to follow that fateful star

1

when it arrived. He drew them near to Him through the stars they worshiped. The Babylonian captivity was a terrible time in the history of Israel, and yet it was also the event God used to connect His prophet with a distant pagan people, setting up a very long-term plan for their journey to Bethlehem. God loved them and reached out to them.

These pagan magi remind us that Christ came first to Israel, but He also came for the whole world; the far-off Gentiles would be saved along with God's own people. The Wise Men's carefully selected gifts signal the holy Infant's true identity. As the Midnight Office for the Nativity of Christ on December 25 proclaims:

> They readily opened their treasures, and they offered Him
>   precious gifts:
> pure gold to the King of the ages; incense to the God of all;
> and myrrh to the immortal One, who would die for three days.
> Come, all nations, let us worship Him who was born to save
>   our souls.[1]

Myrrh for Christ's Humanity

Not all human beings are called to serve as priests, and far fewer will become kings—but every one of us will die. The myrrh is the gift that indicates that Christ is truly human, because He shares the fate that is common to everyone. Jesus is fully God, and we know that He also is fully human because His body is mortal, vulnerable, and weak. He took on a body just like ours.

There is something so important about these corruptible bodies. Jesus is constantly healing our human bodies, feeding them,

---

1   GOA Digital Chant Stand, updated January 2025, Services for December 25, Midnight Office, https://digitalchantstand.goarch.org/goa/dcs/dcs.html.

and caring for them, and—as we've noted—He will judge us by how we have handled the bodies of others. Mother Maria of Paris expresses this idea beautifully:

> The way to God lies through love of people. At the Last Judgment I shall not be asked whether I was successful in my ascetic exercises, nor how many bows and prostrations I made. Instead I shall be asked did I feed the hungry, clothe the naked, visit the sick and the prisoners. That is all I shall be asked. About every poor, hungry and imprisoned person the Savior says 'I': 'I was hungry and thirsty, I was sick and in prison.' To think that he puts an equal sign between himself and anyone in need. . . . I always knew it, but now it has somehow penetrated to my sinews. It fills me with awe.[2]

The "love of people" is not manifested in words or in grand gestures, but in the very simple acts of mercy that minister to the body: giving food and drink, attending to the sick and the lonely and the captives.

Christ loves us so much that He merges with us; He identifies with the hungry, the sick, the downtrodden. Our Creator takes on flesh, and the Master becomes a servant. The heavenly Physician and great Healer identifies with the patient, with the injured and the ill, and asks *us* to be the healers who will serve His Body.

Jesus' years on earth begin and end with myrrh: the Magi, representative of all those peoples He has come to save, will present Him with myrrh at His birth; He'll be twice anointed before His death; and early on that glorious Sunday morning, the myrrh-bearing women will approach His Tomb, ready to minister to His body with myrrh once more. The myrrh is always the generous gift that points to His mortality and to His anointing as the King of

---

2   Sergei Hackel, *Pearl of Great Price: The Life of Mother Maria Skobtsova 1891–1945* (St. Vladimir's Seminary Press, 1965), 29.

Kings—and myrrh becomes the sweet fragrance of the love we offer one another, as we care for each other throughout our march toward death and to the life that lies beyond it.

FOR REFLECTION

- It is often said that the one experience all human beings have in common is death, and when Jesus takes on humanity, He also takes on death. In what ways does mortality bring us together? In what ways does it keep us apart?

- In his Letter to the Hebrews, Paul writes, "Inasmuch then as the children have partaken of flesh and blood, He Himself likewise shared in the same, that through death He might destroy him who had the power of death, that is, the devil, and release those who through fear of death were all their lifetime subject to bondage" (Heb. 2:14–15). How does the fear of death limit us and hold us in bondage?

- In ways mysterious and unknown to us, God reaches out to all of humanity, in every corner of the world—and He calls on us, wherever we are and whoever we meet, to lovingly serve our neighbor. How can you answer that call today—both for those within your own circle, and those who are outside?

Part One

THE HOLY MYRRHBEARERS

MARY, THE MOTHER
OF GOD

The Virgin Mary surely is the best known of the myrrhbearing women, and she is truly Christ's myrrhbearer in every sense of the word: From the beginning to the end of His life, she was always there, taking care of Him. She cared for Jesus as an infant and as He grew into a young man, and when He set out for His public ministry, she was among the "many others who provided for Him from their substance" (Luke 8:3). And at the end of His earthly life, she remained with Him at His Crucifixion and came to His Tomb to care for His body after death. She is both His myrrhbearer and a myrrhbearer to all of us, for as Christ's mother she is a mother to His Body, the Church.

Mary's Birth and Early Years

Mary's parents, Joachim and Anna, the grandparents of our Lord, were a very faithful couple.[1] It is said that Joachim raised sheep—

---

1   The Church preserves many details from the Protoevangelion of James about the Virgin Mary's birth, childhood, and betrothal to the Righteous Joseph. Although not a part of the canonical Scriptures, the Proto-evangelion is much beloved and is a source of hymnography and Holy Tradition about the Theotokos. All extrabiblical details about the Virgin Mary and Righteous Joseph are drawn from the Protoevangelion and *The Life of the Virgin Mary, the Theotokos* (Holy Apostles Convent, 1989).

including lambs used for sacrifice—and that he was both prosperous and generous, giving one third of what he had to the temple and another third to the poor. Despite their piety and general goodness, the couple was barren. Because children are a gift from God, for the Jewish people it naturally followed that barrenness was a kind of curse, a judgment leveled by God on those who were undeserving. As Joachim and Anna grew older and still no babies were granted them, they must have felt increasingly saddened and frustrated.

During one great annual feast, when they had reached their elderly years, Joachim brought their offering to the temple and was turned away: The priest Reuben declared that the childless man was not worthy to offer a sacrifice to God. Joachim was crushed, as was Anna when she heard. In their pain, the couple parted—they went away to pray and to process this terrible judgment independently. Each in their solitude began to pray most earnestly for a child, and an angel appeared, announcing that indeed, this very old woman would conceive a daughter who would be blessed above all other women. The angel instructed them to dedicate her to life in the temple, that she might be a faithful servant of God.

Joachim and Anna came back together with great joy, and indeed they conceived a daughter. When Mary was born, Anna followed the tradition of so many prayerful women who were childless: Like Hannah, she praised God for this much-desired blessing, and when the child was around three years old, Joachim and Anna brought her to the temple, where she would grow up serving God.[2] Tradition holds that little Mary ran joyfully (or "danced with her feet") up the temple steps to begin her new life in

---

2   Hannah's story of her struggle with fertility and her fervent prayers is
     told in 1 Samuel 1:2—2:21. She too is blessed with a child and delivers
     Samuel to be raised with the priest Eli at the tabernacle.

the temple.[3] She was one of several young women there, all being educated in the Faith, attending prayer services, and working on various crafts for the temple, such as spinning thread and weaving cloth.[4] Mary was especially prayerful and stood out among the girls for her gentleness.

When the girls came of age, they could no longer live in the temple, and they returned to their families to prepare for marriage. But by the time Mary turned thirteen, her parents, who were quite elderly when she was born, had passed away. The obvious solution was to find a husband for her, but Mary objected, saying, "It cannot be that I should know a man or that a man should know me."[5] Her parents had devoted her to a life serving God, and she privately had vowed never to marry. The Jewish community assumed that all young women would marry and hope to be blessed with a large family, but Mary had settled on something else entirely: a life of chastity, of perpetual virginity. She could not, however, stay in the temple. A woman properly could live with her father, her husband, or her son—and Mary had none of these. She had inherited her father's property, but this did not free her to live on her own; it simply meant that legally she had to marry a man from her own tribe to prevent the property from transferring to another tribe.

---

3   See Protoevangelion of James 7.

4   *The Life of the Virgin Mary* notes that we don't have much information on how such girls lived, but apparently parents would sometimes consecrate daughters to temple service, where "they received a proper education in the doctrines, commandments, and sacred rites of their religion" (60).

5   As cited in *The Life of the Virgin Mary, the Theotokos*; the text continues, explaining, "She assigned the following reasons for her resolve to remain a virgin: that both she and her parents had devoted her to the service of the Lord and that she herself had vowed never to lie with a man" (60). Saint Gregory of Nyssa is cited as explaining that Mary vowed "to remain untouched and to entirely dedicate her flesh as a sacred offering to God" (63). Because of her vow, Mary is especially dear to monastics and is considered the patroness of Mt. Athos.

The high priest did not demand that Mary relinquish her stubborn vow to God but instead found a way to allow it. He gathered with the council, and they agreed to betroth her to a righteous man from her tribe. With this arrangement, the man would take legal responsibility for her, but as they were not married, they would never consummate their union. The men cast lots to see who would be given this responsibility, and it fell to Joseph, a carpenter whose wife of forty years had died just the year before.

While many people celebrated that God had chosen him to receive the young woman who some believed to be the likely mother of the coming messiah,[6] Joseph was concerned. His grandchildren were older than Mary, and he worried about looking ridiculous. But he obeyed, thinking that perhaps he would marry her to one of his sons. The high priest corrected him: The only person who could be betrothed to Mary was Joseph himself.

In Joseph's Home

Joseph's home was probably quite lively. He and his wife, Salome, had seven children—James, Jude, Simon, Joses, Salome, Esther, and one other daughter. Despite the fact that his children and grandchildren were around to keep Mary company, Joseph asked

---

6   In *The Life of the Virgin Mary, the Theotokos*, the authors examine historical accounts and hymnology which indicate that Mary was already known as the one through whom God would "make manifest His redemption unto the children of Israel" (33). They note that Anna "clearly knew of her daughter's place in the history of redemption" (32) and assert that "all the house of Israel loved her" (33). Mary would spend many hours every day in the Holy of Holies, off limits to all others except for one priest on the annual Day of Atonement, specifically because God "foreordained the holy Virgin to become the supreme 'holy of holies'" by bearing God; just "as the Holy of Holies was filled with the glory of God's presence—so much that the priests could not bear the glory of it—so the womb of the all-holy Virgin was to be filled with the glory of God's presence" (49).

the high priests if five of the temple virgins could join her. The high priest agreed, and Mary moved into Joseph's home in Nazareth, accompanied by Rebecca, Sepphora, Susanna, Abigail, and Jael. Shortly thereafter, Joseph left, as he routinely spent many months abroad working on houses. Mary and the other girls were not bored, for the high priest assigned them a job: They were to spin the thread for a new temple veil. (This is the very veil, it is said, that ripped in the earthquake that occurred when Mary's Son died on the Cross.)[7]

While she was spinning this thread, Mary was approached by the Archangel Gabriel, bringing the news that she would bear the Son of God. Mary earnestly agreed, and it is fair to say that her entire life changed in that moment. Indeed, the very direction of the universe changed. But Mary's life had always been on course to serve God, to offer up her body and her life to Him—though now her intentions were to be fulfilled in an astonishing way.

Mary's *yes*, and to all it would entail—the wild unknown of the angel's strange words, the potential for shame and humiliation, the difficulties and dangers of pregnancy and childbirth—would set salvation in motion, reversing the moment when Eve's refusal to obey God ushered in sin and death. As St. Irenaeus so beautifully observed, "The knot of Eve's disobedience was loosed by the obedience of Mary. For what the virgin Eve had bound fast through unbelief, this did the virgin Mary set free through faith."[8] At the moment when Mary said yes, everything changed, as God Himself took on flesh (her flesh, really), becoming Man.

By becoming the Mother of God, Mary became the source of the Incarnation, because God took on Mary's flesh, with her DNA.

---

7   *Life of the Virgin Mary*, 64–66.

8   St. Irenaeus, *Against Heresies*, bk. 3, chap. 22, trans. Alexander Roberts and William Rambaut, Ante-Nicene Fathers, vol. 1, rev. ed., ed. Kevin Knight (New Advent), https://www.newadvent.org/fathers/0103322.htm.

Mary offered her body in a unique and tangible way, hosting God in her womb, a gift to all mankind. There is nothing abstract about Mary's offering. Christ's love is not expressed in the abstract: He expressed it concretely on the Cross. Mary's commitment to God is concrete and physical, a literal offering of her own body. Christian love is incarnate love. The love you and I offer must take on flesh too. Our actions must come to *embody* love in the simplest and most practical ways. In this sense, we might think of Christian service, of myrrhbearing, as *love incarnate.*

The Magnificat

When next we see Mary, a few months have passed and she has traveled into the hill country to visit her cousin, Elizabeth. Saint Luke records her very poetic outpouring of praise, the Magnificat, which gives us beautiful insight into Mary's joyful experience of pregnancy. Her words convey her humility and her deep love of God:

> My soul magnifies the Lord,
> And my spirit has rejoiced in God my Savior.
> For He has regarded the lowly state of His maidservant;
> For behold, henceforth all generations will call me blessed.
>   (Luke 1:46–48)

Mary's words move from her own experience of God's mercy and love to His defense of the lowly and the hungry, and culminate in His wonderful care for Israel. Her words reveal that Mary is well educated in the Faith, deeply prayerful, and filled with the grace of God. (And how could she be anything but filled with grace, as she carries God Himself in her womb?)

Saint Luke offers us a vision of Mary that is on the one hand eloquent and poetic, and on the other, quiet and watchful. At the birth of our Savior, though she is of course central to the event, she does not speak, and there is only one reference to her inner experience: "But Mary kept all these things and pondered them in her heart" (Luke 2:19). She receives the shepherds' words about her Child but says not a thing. Forty days later, when the elderly Simeon offered his prophecy in the temple, both Joseph and Mary silently "marveled," keeping quiet even when Simeon said that "a sword would pierce" Mary's very soul (Luke 2:33–35).

Imagine having access to Mary's private contemplations, to the prayerful pondering of her heart. Her faith and her understanding of God were clearly profound and vast and only could have been made more so by her close contact with Him. We know that pregnancy changes a woman both physically and emotionally, but how much more so when the Child she carries is her Creator? Perhaps it is better that we do not know exactly what she was thinking, as the silence invites us to contemplate the importance of the ways in which we too carry Christ within us.

Mary's Vigilance

We catch an unusually clear and interesting glimpse of the Theotokos in the second chapter of the Gospel of St. John, when he describes the wedding at Cana:

> On the third day there was a wedding in Cana of Galilee, and the mother of Jesus was there. Now both Jesus and his disciples were invited to the wedding. And when they ran out of wine, the mother of Jesus said to Him, "They have no wine."
>
> Jesus said to her, "Woman, what does your concern have to do with Me? My hour has not yet come."
>
> His mother said to the servants, "Whatever He says to you, do *it.*" (John 2:1–5)

From this short passage, we learn that Mary sat quietly and watched: She was observing more closely than other guests, and even more closely than the man in charge, who never suspected that the wedding feast had nearly run out of wine (John 2:9–10). While others are distracted with the party, Mary monitors the situation carefully and compassionately. Her disposition is quiet but vigilant: She watches over the wedding feast, and when she sees a problem on the horizon, she takes action.

In his homily on this miracle, St. John Chrysostom said that Mary "knew that His refusal proceeded not from want of power, but from humility, and that He might not seem without cause to hurry to the miracle; and therefore she brought the servants."[9] According to St. John, Mary knew that Jesus was open to providing miraculous wine for this couple but didn't want to draw attention to Himself. Mary knew her Son well enough to understand what He was thinking, and she directed the servants to follow His instructions. She knew that He would provide the wine, even though it was not yet time for public miracles.

Myrrhbearing as Practical, Incarnate Love

It is intriguing that in the very first miracle the Gospels record, Jesus does not heal a blind man or make a paralytic walk. His action seems such a small thing: The wedding celebration might have run out of wine, so the Mother of God intervenes, insisting that her Son smooth the way for the festivities, making the joy of the new couple and their parents complete. Preserving their joy mattered to her. This glimpse of Mary, quiet and alert to the

---

9   St. John Chrysostom, "Homily 22 on the Gospel of John," trans. Charles Marriott, in *Nicene and Post-Nicene Fathers, First Series*, vol. 14, rev. ed., ed. Kevin Knight (New Advent), https://www.newadvent.org/fathers/240122.htm.

struggles of others, is a wonderful foreshadowing of who she is today in the life of the Church. When people pray for her help, Mary always delivers. Surely no single saint is called upon more frequently or successfully to intercede, for Mary cares about preserving not just the life, but the joy, of every person.

FOR REFLECTION

- From age three, Mary's life was given over to the service of God. What would change about your life if you were to offer yourself so completely to Him?

- Mary, while eloquent, was generally quiet, pondering things in her heart and watching for needs she might fill. In icons, as is true of other saints, she usually is shown with a small mouth and large ears, for she listened more than she spoke. How might our own stillness open up the possibility of seeing needs we might otherwise miss?

- What do you make of the fact that Christ said He would not do this miracle, but His mother pressed onward, and only then did He submit? What does this tell us about intercessory prayer?

MARY MAGDALENE

All four Gospels mention Mary Magdalene by name, and she is first in most lists of the women who financially supported Jesus' journeys (Luke 8:2–3), ministered to Him, stayed with Him at the Cross,[1] and approached His Tomb on the day of His Resurrection. The name *Magdalene* indicates that she was from Magdala, a town on the western coast of the Sea of Galilee located between Tiberias, where St. Peter often fished, and Capernaum, where he lived. We know that her parents, Syros and Efharistia, were pious Jews with a highly developed sense of charity and compassion, which they transmitted to their daughter.[2] Mary was a woman of means who helped fund Christ and His ministries.

The primary biographical fact that both Saints Luke and Mark give about Mary Magdalene is that Jesus drove seven demons out of her (Luke 8:2–3; Mark 16:9). It's a tantalizing detail, especially for modern audiences. What does this mean?

---

1   Mary Magdalene is listed first in the Gospels of Mark (15:40, 47; 16:1), Matthew (27:56, 61; 28:1), and Luke (24:10). Only St. John puts her last: "Now there stood by the cross of Jesus His mother, and His mother's sister, Mary the wife of Clopas, and Mary Magdalene" (John 19:25). However, he names her as the only woman to come to Christ's Tomb on the morning of His Resurrection.

2   *Holy Myrrh-Bearer Mary Magdalen, Equal of the Apostles: Life, Service, & Akathist Hymn*, trans. Isaac E. Lambertsen, 2nd ed. (The St. John of Kronstadt Press, 1999).

Seven is a significant number in the Scriptures: It signals completion, perfection. A person taken over by seven demons would be thoroughly given over to evil. We might try to imagine for a moment what she felt like—captive, helpless to fight these dark powers within her. Other saints who served Satan, like St. Cyprian, were attracted to demonic promises of great power, and when they saw how much greater our Lord's power is, they immediately chose to follow Jesus. Mary Magdalene would have simultaneously come into contact with Christ's great power and felt the sudden exhilaration of freedom as the demons left her. Scholars debate whether we are to take this literally, or to understand that she was somehow metaphorically subject to seven demonic influences or powers— but, of course, we may never understand exactly how this worked. Nevertheless, this profound experience compelled her to become Jesus' disciple and His patron.

Unfortunately, in Western tradition, Mary Magdalene often is wrongly identified as the sinful woman who anointed Christ's feet with perfume before His Passion: This anonymous woman "stood at His feet behind *Him* weeping; and she began to wash His feet with her tears, and wiped *them* with the hair of her head; and she kissed His feet and anointed *them* with the fragrant oil" (Luke 7:38).

Probably because Jesus had cast seven demons out of her, many in the West have conflated Mary with this unnamed and repentant harlot. There is, of course, no reason to connect the two, since Mary Magdalene often is identified by name, but the sinful woman is unnamed and perhaps even unknown to the disciples. The text does say that the repentant woman was "in that town" where Jesus was visiting, and as far as we can tell, that town is Nain—not Magdala. (And, of course, the woman who washed Jesus' feet with her tears is a myrrhbearing woman herself, for she anoints the Body of our Lord.)

After remaining with Christ along with the other women throughout His Crucifixion and burial, according to St. John, when they returned the next morning, Mary Magdalene was the first person to see and interact with Jesus in His resurrected state:

Jesus said to her, "Mary!"

She turned and said to Him, "Rabboni!" (which is to say, Teacher).

Jesus said to her, "Do not cling to Me, for I have not yet ascended to My Father; but go to My brethren and say to them, 'I am ascending to My Father and your Father, and *to* My God and your God.'"

Mary Magdalene came and told the disciples that she had seen the Lord, and *that* He had spoken these things to her. (John 20:16–18)

From that morning forward, Mary never stopped preaching Christ's Resurrection and Ascension. In the years to follow, she would travel far and wide, preaching Christ's gospel so effectively that she has been given the title, "Equal to the Apostles."

Evangelism

Mary Magdalene traveled with Mary the wife of Clopas to Rome in AD 34, but along their way, they are said to have visited the Greek island of Zakynthos. They were the very first people to preach Christ on this island; women who had borne myrrh for Christ now bore the gospel, bringing the Good News to places where God was unknown. What must it have felt like for the two Maries to land on a strange island, bearing the greatest news of all time, but also uncertain about how they'd be received? They could easily be embraced or attacked, welcomed or killed by angry mobs.

The two women faced real danger, and their efforts were rewarded. Today, Zakynthos is filled with Christians and has produced great saints. Festivals celebrate Mary Magdalene's arrival there, and locals point to the specific location where the women disembarked, saying that Mary Magdalene's footprint is still visible on the shore. A village on the island is named Maries in honor of the two Maries who carried the gospel to their shores.

After Zakynthos, Mary Magdalene continued to Rome and visited Emperor Tiberias to proclaim Christ's Resurrection to him. As it was customary to bring a gift for the emperor, she brought him an egg. According to Church Tradition, she told him the story of Jesus' Crucifixion and Resurrection, and the emperor exclaimed that a resurrected man was about as likely as the egg in her hand turning red—and then the egg did, in fact, turn red. While the emperor did not drop to his knees to convert, Christians were impressed enough to keep the tradition of dying red eggs at Pascha for two millennia. The Akathist to St. Mary Magdalene proclaims,

When thou didst meet with the Emperor Tiberius, thou gavest him a red-coloured egg to represent the Resurrection, and thou didst say, "Christ is Risen." It is for this cause that, to this day and in churches all over the world, the faithful give eggs on the Feast of the Resurrection. Thou art illustrious and commendable, Saint Mary Magdalene, and we praise thy wondrous life and thank God for thy marvelous labours.[3]

According to Tradition, Mary Magdalene remained in Rome until the arrival of the Apostle Paul and stayed for two more years

---

3   *The Akathist to the Holy Myrrhbearer and Equal to the Apostles St. Mary Magdalene* can be found at the website of St. Mary Magdalene Orthodox Church in Fenton, MI, http://www.st-marymagdalene.org/st-mary-magdalene.

after he left Rome the first time. Growing older, she moved to Ephesus, where the holy Apostle John lived. She preached with John and lived out her remaining years there. She is remembered as a loyal friend to Christ whose gratitude for His healing love was never extinguished; she offered up her fortune and her life in thanksgiving, and followed Him to the end of her days.

FOR REFLECTION

- The number seven indicates completeness or fullness, as God created the heavens and the earth (and found time to rest) in seven days. When we read that Christ cast out seven demons from Mary Magdalene, we understand that she was completely given over to darkness and evil—and yet, Christ found her worthy of healing and completely changed her life. Each of us struggles with darkness in our own way. Is it ever hard to have faith that Christ will find us worthy of healing and that He can actually accomplish it if we trust in Him?

- Mary Magdalene's dedication to Christ was likely proportionate to the healing she received from Him. Are we always aware of the healing and deliverance Christ grants us? Do we respond with this kind of dedication?

- Mary was a woman of means who used her fortune to support Jesus and His mission. It is easy to imagine doing such a thing, if He were with us in person today, and yet, we pass up opportunities to support the ministries of the Body of Christ. What do you think Mary had that we don't have?

MARY, THE WIFE
OF CLOPAS

In St. John's Gospel we read that "there stood by the cross of Jesus His mother, and His mother's sister, Mary the wife of Clopas, and Mary Magdalene" (John 19:25). Holy Tradition holds that Jesus' mother, Mary, was an only child—the much-prayed-for daughter who came late in life to Joachim and Anna. How, then, can John say that she had a sister? We can assume that John is referring to Mary's sister-in-law, for Clopas (which, when translated into English, is variously spelled Clopas, Cleopas, and Cleophas) was Joseph's younger brother.[1] The brother's wife, Mary, would have been sister-in-law to the Theotokos and aunt to Jesus. Standing by the Cross with the mother of God and Mary Magdalene, she was witnessing the cruel death of her Lord and her nephew, whom she may have known since His infancy.

Of course, her husband, Clopas (Cleopas), appears in the Scriptures as well: Luke tells us that on the day of Christ's Resurrection,

---

1   Eusebius's *Historia Ecclesiastica, Book III, Chapter XI*. Written between AD 312 and 324, this was the first important work of Christian history since the Acts of the Apostles. Eusebius is quoting Hegesippus, a Palestinian historian who interviewed some of Jesus' surviving relatives. Eusebius claimed that Hegesippus wrote his *Memoirs* in his old age, during the reign of Pope Eleutherius (AD 175–189). In addition, Epiphanius indicates that Joseph and Cleopas were brothers, sons of "Jacob, surnamed Panther."

he and "the one whose name was Cleopas" were walking to Emmaus when the resurrected Jesus drew near and began to speak with them, though "their eyes were restrained, so that they did not know Him" (Luke 24:13–35). It was Clopas who turned to the Lord, asking incredulously, "Are You the only stranger in Jerusalem, and have You not known the things which happened there in these days?" They described the Crucifixion and the discovery of the empty Tomb, and our Lord expounded what the Law Moses, the Prophets, and the writings said about Him (Luke 24:27–32). Luke and Clopas were not among the chosen twelve, and yet they were the ones to whom our Lord explained the plan of salvation.

These men were both apostles, sent out as part of the Seventy that Christ sent two by two into every city He was about to visit, preparing His way (Luke 10:1–24). In the years following Christ's Ascension, Clopas continued to preach the gospel,[2] until he met his untimely end: He was martyred for His apostolic fervor, in his own home in Emmaus—the very house where he had once seen our Lord in the breaking of the bread.[3]

A Family Following Christ

As family and as dedicated disciples of our Lord, Mary and Clopas were an integral part of Jesus' inner circle. Clopas was a dedicated apostle, traveling and preaching, healing the sick, and finding that "even the demons are subject to us in Your name" (Luke 10:17). They

---

2   According to Hippolytus, in "The Same Hippolytus on the Seventy Apostles," Clopas served as bishop of Jerusalem; however, Eusebius does not include him in his list of early bishops of Jerusalem, which includes the dates they served and leaves no room for Clopas. Perhaps Hippolytus is confused, because Clopas's son Simeon was the second bishop of Jerusalem.

3   For information on Clopas, see both the Roman *Martyrology* and St. Demetrius of Rostov's *Great Collection of the Lives of the Saints*, vol. 5, for January 4: "Saint Cleopas, Younger Brother of Joseph the Betrothed."

both left their home in Emmaus to travel, perhaps together some-times but also separately. Clopas partnered with another apostle, and Mary with the women, learning from Christ and providing for Him.

Mary's children also were part of this inner circle, for in the Gospels of Matthew and Mark she is identified as the mother of James and Joseph / Joses (Matt. 27:56; Mark 15:40–41).[4] She likely watched Jesus grow up with her boys. Her brother-in-law Joseph served as the protector of Jesus in His early years, and Clopas, Joseph's younger brother, walked from town to town, telling the people that his nephew, the Son of God, was on His way to show them the Kingdom. Their children followed Christ, and James was one of the twelve. The entire family was following Him and sup-porting Him.

Instead of ascending Israel's throne, our Lord ascended a cross and died, and Mary's whole life was on the line. Everything and everyone she had was tied up in Jesus' ministry. Her entire family was at risk. If this amazing and beautiful time with Jesus simply came to humiliation and defeat, what would that mean? Where would they go? And yet, Mary was there as the sun rose on Sunday morning, with arms full of myrrh and spices, because she loved Jesus. Where else would she be?

After the Lord's Ascension, Mary and Clopas were a vital part of the early Church, and their son Simeon served as the second bishop of Jerusalem. The couple continued to live in the nearby town of Emmaus, in the home where they entertained Christ. Eventually, men violated the sanctity of their home to murder

---

4　James is described as the son of Alphaeus (not of Clopas) when three of the Gospel writers list the names of the Twelve (Matt. 10:3, Mark 3:18, Luke 6:15). Orthodox Tradition generally holds that Alphaeus is an Aramaic version of the name Clopas, which would make all these the children of Clopas and Mary, cousins to our Lord. (This is specifically asserted by Papias of Hierapolis, *Exposition of the Sayings of the Lord, Fragment X,* earlychristianwritings.com, and others.)

Clopas for his refusal to hide his great love of Christ. He would be buried there in their home, where he was born.

Eventually Mary traveled to Rome with another faithful Myrrhbearer, Mary Magdalene, by way of the Greek island of Zakynthos. We don't know what came of her after that, but what a remarkable legacy, to share credit for bringing the gospel to the future home of a holy saint like St. Dionysios the Wonderworker. In addition to being a myrrhbearer at Christ's holy Tomb, and the wife and mother of apostles, Mary herself is part of the apostolic history of the Church, having preached the gospel of Christ on Zakynthos and we know not where else.

FOR REFLECTION

- The lives of Orthodox saints sometimes feature couples who, in their later years, amicably split apart to enter separate monasteries. (Indeed, wives have historically been asked to take orders so that their husbands could serve as bishops.) Mary and Clopas seem to have parted so they could better serve Christ, with Clopas going out among the Seventy and Mary traveling with the women. Is it surprising that Christ would call a married couple to serve separately?

- It is likely that Mary had known Christ since He was a child. What do you suppose was going through her mind as she stood beside His mother at the Crucifixion?

- Mary's husband, Clopas, was killed in their home, but rather than abandon Christ in fear, she pushed on, traveling to far-away lands to spread the gospel. Yet on some days, we have trouble leaving the comfort of our homes to go to Liturgy. Could God be calling you to more "going out" than you're doing? What holds you back?

SALOME

Among the many women who followed Christ, ministering to Him, was Salome. You may know her as the mother who approached Jesus with a bold request, gathering her sons, James and John, and bringing them before the Lord:

> Then the mother of Zebedee's sons came to Him with her sons, kneeling down and asking something from Him.
>
> And He said to her, "What do you wish?"
>
> She said to Him, "Grant that these two sons of mine may sit, one on Your right hand and the other on the left, in Your kingdom." (Matt. 20:20–21)

Many readers will find Salome strangely pushy and interfering, but perhaps her request makes more sense when we understand who Salome was to our Lord. As the daughter of St. Joseph the Beloved, she was in effect Jesus' aunt, who had known Him all His life. The apostles she put forth for promotion were His cousins, His lifelong playmates and trusted friends. She saw her grown sons placed in prominent positions among the twelve chosen disciples: Along with Peter, James and John were chosen to witness both the Transfiguration of our Lord and the raising of Jairus's daughter when other disciples were sent away (Mark 9:2; 5:37). In light of their close relationship, perhaps we can be more sympathetic to her request.

Hers was a fairly common name, so we must take care not to confuse this Salome with the various others who appear in Scripture—such as the one who served as a midwife at Christ's birth, or Herod's niece, who demanded the head of St. John the Forerunner on a platter. Blessed Theophylact of Ochrid explains who exactly this Salome is: "The mother of the sons of Zebedee was named Salome. They say that she also was a daughter of Joseph."[1] Of course, the Scriptures are clear that in addition to His "brothers," Jesus was blessed with sisters, for Matthew tells us that in His own hometown, the residents murmured, "Is this not the carpenter's son? Is not His mother called Mary? And His brothers James, Joses, Simon, and Judas? And His sisters, are they not all with us?" (Matt. 13:55–56). Joseph had both sons and daughters, all of whom comprised Jesus' extended family.

Salome in Her Father's Home

As we have noted, Tradition holds that Joseph and his first wife, Salome, for whom this Salome was named, had seven children. After Joseph's wife died, Mary came into the household. She and Salome surely spent time together and perhaps even grew close.

Consider for a moment what Salome's life was like. We can imagine that Joseph was a caring father and that her many siblings filled some of the void when her mother passed away. Then Joseph came home from a meeting at the temple, troubled. He announced that he would be bringing a young woman and her five friends into

---

1   Bl. Theophylact, *The Explanation of the Holy Gospel According to St. Matthew* 27.56, trans. Rev. Fr. Christopher Stade, Bl. Theophylact's Explanation of the New Testament, vol. 1 (St. Herman of Alaska Brotherhood /Chrysostom Press, 1992).

the household. Within a short time, this new member of the family was suddenly with child, though without an identifiable father. Mary and Joseph both were visited by the angel whose promises inspired and reassured them, but what about Salome? She had to trust their word—that their angelic visions were real and that the child coming to be born in their own household was sent by God.

Life as Wife and Mother

At some point Salome was given in marriage to a fisherman named Zebedee. Jesus would nickname their sons *Boanerges,* or the "Sons of Thunder" (Mark 3:17). What does that nickname mean? Are we to understand that the brothers are thunderous, quick to anger? Or could this be a reference to their father? They're sons of Zebedee, and sons of Thunder. Did Zebedee have a temper? Did his anger rumble through the home? Perhaps the brothers took after their father, and the whole household would sometimes explode in anger. We do know that St. Luke tells us that, at one point, James and John offered to "command fire to come down from heaven and consume" some Samaritans (Luke 9:54).

On the other hand, Church Fathers often have suggested that Christ's use of *thunder* refers to the power of the brothers' future preaching. Consider, for instance, the very powerful words opening the Gospel of John: "In the beginning was the Word, and the Word was with God, and the Word was God." In a homily on John's Gospel, Saint John Chrysostom notes that these words resonate like thunder:

> What zeal, what earnestness ought you in reason to display, when it is no musician or debater who now comes forward to a trial of skill, but when a man is speaking from heaven, and utters a voice plainer than thunder? For he has pervaded the whole earth with

the sound; and occupied and filled it, not by the loudness of the cry, but by moving his tongue with the grace of God.[2]

The Fathers remind us that God's voice thunders from heaven; His divine voice is loud and powerful, and so are the messages that two of the greatest apostles, James and John the Beloved, would deliver.

Zebedee and his boys partnered with Peter (Luke 5:10) in a fishing business successful enough to support multiple employees. Luke tells us that Jesus came to them one day when they were fishing and, after preaching from Peter's boat, He told them to put out a bit farther. They obeyed, though they'd fished all day with nothing to show for it, and they brought in a tremendous catch. But Jesus called them to more than a successful livelihood, telling Simon, "From now on you will catch men." In response they brought their boats back to land, and "they forsook all and followed Him" (Luke 5:9–11). They even left their own father behind in response to Jesus' call (Mark 1:19–20).

While it's tempting to imagine that Zebedee was frustrated with his sons' departure, we should remember that Jesus was no stranger. He was family, and when the boys left, Salome followed Him too. What's more, they don't seem to have left home permanently: At various times after being called, Peter would be found fishing again, surely in the same boats and with his same partner, Zebedee. Salome and the other women were financially supporting Jesus' ministry, so perhaps Zebedee ran the business for Peter and his boys while they were away with Jesus, and the profits were dedicated to supporting Jesus' ministries on earth.

---

2   St. John Chrysostom, from preface to "Homily on John 1," trans. Charles Marriott and ed. Philip Schaff in *Nicene and Post-Nicene Fathers, First Series*, vol. 14, rev. ed., ed. Kevin Knight (New Advent), https://www.newadvent.org/fathers/240101.htm.

Whoever Desires to Become Great

Jesus does not rebuke Salome and her sons, but He points out that they "do not know what [they] ask" and cannot "drink the cup that [He is] about to drink, and be baptized with the baptism that [He is] baptized with" (Matt. 20:22). It simply would not be possible for His cousins to rule with Him.

While the other disciples are scandalized by Salome's bold request and upset with James and John for hoping for an elevated position, Jesus' response seems to be equally directed at all His followers:

> "You know that the rulers of the Gentiles lord it over them, and those who are great exercise authority over them. Yet it shall not be so among you; but whoever desires to become great among you, let him be your servant. And whoever desires to be first among you, let him be your slave—just as the Son of Man did not come to be served, but to serve, and to give His life as a ransom for many." (Matt. 20:25–28)

Christ's response is directed not just to His aunt and cousins; He takes this opportunity to teach all the apostles the paradox of servant leadership, that the best leaders will not wield power proudly to dominate but will serve with the humblest of hearts. This would be a lesson Salome and her sons would not soon forget in the coming years; each of them would offer themselves up as true servants of Christ, without any further concern for position or status.

Salome's legacy includes her sons, both of whom were among the twelve holy apostles. Of course, John was particularly distinguished among the Twelve: Christ entrusted him with the care of His own mother. In his later years, John wrote a Gospel, three epistles, and the Apocalypse (the Book of Revelation), and is one of only three people honored by the Church with the designation of *Theologian*.

Salome's sons had their mother's blessing: When they left home to follow Christ, she didn't try to hold them back, but instead she joined the other women who provided for Jesus and His disciples, traveling along with them. Knowing that Jesus was hated by the chief priests and the scribes, that it was dangerous to stand beside Him, she asked Him to put her beloved sons on the front lines of the battle, at His right and left hand. So often, we grasp at our family, hoping to keep everyone safe at all costs, but Salome bravely offered her sons and herself to our Lord without hesitation.

FOR REFLECTION

• When Salome's sons left their home and work to follow Christ, though He was targeted by the authorities, Salome did not hold them back out of fear. She even joined them. In much less dramatic ways, we hold back. Why is it so hard for us to be "all in"?

• Salome asked Jesus to seat her sons at His right and left hands. Like the disciples, we often think of her request as ambitious and audacious. Knowing that Christ was hated by the authorities, was there also something brave and sacrificial in it?

• Christ responded to her request with an important lesson: "the first shall be last and the last shall be first." How does Christ see ambition? How do you see it?

SUSANNA

Susanna is mentioned by name just once in the Gospels:

> And the twelve *were* with Him, and certain women who had
> been healed of evil spirits and infirmities—Mary called Magda-
> lene, out of whom had come seven demons, and Joanna the wife
> of Chuza, Herod's steward, and Susanna, and many others who
> provided for Him from their substance. (Luke 8:1–3)

Nothing else is known about Susanna. Like Mary Magdalene,
she is among those who were healed by Jesus, and she is one of the
many women who financially supported His ministry. From this,
we can surmise that Susanna was a wealthy woman from Galilee.
Her gratitude and faith propelled her to dedicate her life and her
fortune to Christ and to follow Him. Although she is not named
in the Gospel accounts of the women who stood near the Cross
and who approached the Tomb early Sunday morning, the Church
honors her as one of the Holy Myrrhbearers, with the understanding that she was one of "the women who followed Him from Galilee" (Luke 23:49).

We don't know what infirmity Susanna suffered from, but we
know that her options for healing were extremely limited compared to our medical care today. We live in a world where science
accomplishes wonders, always growing and pushing boundaries.

Rapidly evolving and increasingly successful medical treatments are the norm for us. Indeed, if there is no good treatment for your friend's disease today, you might counsel patience: Science is sure to cure this any day now! Given the time, money, and access, it feels like just about anything can be cured.

But first-century Galilee was very different. Susanna would have had neither the diagnostic means to pinpoint the cause of her illness, nor the optimism that a medical breakthrough would provide a solution for her. Disease and illness were common, mortality rates were high, and cures were rare. New symptoms of any condition were either ominous, signaling death's arrival, or the new normal to which a sick person must adjust.

Susanna required healing. Her suffering was real. When Jesus came to her in Galilee, she may well have thought, along with so many others, "Is this not Joseph's son?" (Luke 4:22). And yet, there He was, surrounded by crowds eager to hear what He had to say and to see what He would do. Did He approach Susanna with mercy and love in His eyes? Or did she run to Him, asking for His help? We don't know exactly how the story unfolded, but we understand that Christ's gift of healing was no metaphor; our Lord truly and permanently changed the course of her life when He intervened by healing Susanna. His love for her took on a physical expression with this tremendous gift, and her response was equally concrete: She left her home and served Christ and His disciples with both her hands and her financial resources. Susanna's gratitude is expressed in physical service and unwavering faith.

FOR REFLECTION

- Susanna is almost a blank slate, a figure about whom little is known, which allows us to fill in details imaginatively. Who do you see when you try to imagine her?

- In what ways have you experienced healing from God— whether large or small?

- How did Susanna express her gratitude to Christ for healing her? In what ways has your own gratitude taken shape in your life?

JOANNA

Joanna may be one of the most fascinating myrrhbearing women because of her association with the ruling class of Jerusalem. In recent years, an intriguing archaeological find has shed new light on her identity: In Jerusalem in the 1980s, an ossuary was discovered with the inscription, "Joanna granddaughter of Theophilus the High Priest."[1] These words could have referred to any Joanna, of course, but if the Joanna of Luke's Gospel was the offspring of Theophilus, a number of confusing little details would suddenly fit together very nicely.

Luke names Joanna twice in his Gospel: in his initial list of women who followed Christ from Galilee and in the list of women who told the apostles that Christ had risen (Luke 8:2–3; 24:10). No other Gospel lists her by name. At the same time, Luke is also the only evangelist to address his Gospel to Theophilus (Luke 1:3). It has long been assumed, as St. Ambrose of Milan suggested, that *Theophilus* was just a generic term for any "lover of God." Increasingly, however, scholars suggest that Luke is referring to

---

1   For more information on the very interesting story of the ossuary's discovery, which involved court cases and investigation to discern between fraudulent vandalism and real inscriptions, begin with "The Ossuary of Yehohanah Granddaughter of the High Priest Theophilus" by D. Barag and D. Flusser, *Israel Exploration Journal* 36 (1986): 39–44.

Theophilus ben Ananus, who was the high priest in the second temple in Jerusalem from AD 37 to 41.[2] If Luke is indeed writing to this Theophilus, then it follows logically that he would identify this man's granddaughter by name when other evangelists did not.

High priests came from wealthy, important families, and Theophilus was no exception. His people were among the most influential in Judea in the first century: He was the son of the High Priest Annas, and his brother-in-law was Caiaphas, the high priest before whom Jesus appeared. Joanna, for her part, is known to have been a woman of means, which is consistent with Luke's suggestion that she, along with Susanna and Mary Magdalene, was one of the women "who provided for [Jesus] from their substance" (Luke 8:3). Prominent families cement their positions by marrying their children to other prominent people, and it's likely that Joanna's family considered Chuza a fortunate match because of his position as steward, managing the property of Herod Antipas, the Roman tetrarch of Galilee.

Position and Influence Used to Honor God's Holy Prophet

In his Gospel, St. Matthew tells us that Herod Antipas put Jesus' cousin, St. John the Baptist, "in prison for the sake of Herodias, his brother Philip's wife. Because John had said to him, 'It is not lawful for you to have her'" (Matt. 14:3–4). Jesus loved John and proclaimed that "among those born of women there has not risen one greater than John the Baptist" (Matt. 11:11), yet he was unceremoniously killed during Herod's birthday party:

---

2   As reported in Josephus's *Antiquities of the Jews*, trans. William Whiston, Book IX, 6, https://www.gutenberg.org/files/2848/2848-h/2848-h.htm.

The daughter of Herodias danced before them and pleased Herod. Therefore he promised with an oath to give her whatever she might ask.

So she, having been prompted by her mother, said, "Give me John the Baptist's head here on a platter." . . .

So he sent and had John beheaded in prison. And his head was brought on a platter and given to the girl, and she brought *it* to her mother. Then his disciples came and took away the body and buried it, and went and told Jesus. (Matt. 14:6b–8, 10–12)

The loss of such a good man, God's own prophet and saint, was a terrible blow to Jesus and His followers. The Gospel indicates that John's disciples properly buried his body, affording him a dignified burial after such an ignominious death. But his head was placed on a platter and presented at the party. Tradition holds that, because of her position in the palace as the wife of the steward, Joanna was able to obtain his head secretly.[3] Rather than allow St. John to be disrespected by Herodias and Salome, Joanna discreetly took his head to the Mount of Olives and buried it, serving as myrrhbearer to Christ's beloved cousin.

Joanna Preaches

Joanna remained close to Christ, following Him all the way to His arrest and Crucifixion. She and the other women stood by as He suffered, saw where He was buried, and returned after the Sabbath to take care of His body. After the angel told them that Jesus had risen, Luke tells us, "It was Mary Magdalene, Joanna, Mary the mother of James, and the other women with them, who told these

---

3   https://www.oca.org/saints/lives, "First and second finding of the Honorable Head of the Holy Glorious Prophet, Forerunner, and Baptist of the Lord, John."

things to the apostles" (Luke 24:10). Joanna was one of the very first people to preach the Resurrection, and perhaps she would continue doing so in the years to come.

There is some disagreement over whether Joanna might also have gone by the name of Junia. It was common to have a Hebrew or Aramaic name as well as a Greek name, such as Saul/Paul, Levi/Matthew, Judas/Thaddeus, and perhaps Joanna/Junia and even Chuza/Andronicus. If so, some speculate that they may be the couple mentioned in St. Paul's Letter to the Romans: "Greet Andronicus and Junia, my countrymen and my fellow prisoners, who are of note among the apostles, who also were in Christ before me" (Rom. 16:7). Chuza and Joanna, like Andronicus and Junia, knew Christ before Paul encountered the Lord. This is not, of course, enough confirmation to assure us one way or the other if the woman St. John Chrysostom praised is actually the Myrrhbearer Joanna:

> And indeed to be apostles at all is a great thing. But to be even among these of note, just consider what a great encomium this is! But they were of note owing to their works, to their achievements. Oh! How great is the devotion of this woman, that she should be even counted worthy of the appellation of apostle![4]

Perhaps some day another archaeological find will tell us whether Joanna could be Junia, but until then there is nothing more solid to tie them together. While speculation swirls around archaeological and biographical questions, the fact remains that Joanna has long been honored by the Church for her beautiful service to Christ and to His cousin, John. She was a true myrrhbearer,

---

4   St. John Chrysostom, "Homily 31 on Romans," https://www.newadvent. org/fathers/210231.htm.

risking her position and even her safety to spare John from further indignity by retrieving his head and granting him a respectful burial.[5] At the same time, she was one of the women providing for Christ during His ministry, learning from Him. Soon, she would stand at the foot of the Cross and approach His Tomb at daybreak. If anything, the more we learn about Joanna's family associations, the more we understand that she had a lot to lose. As a member of an influential Jewish family married to a Roman official, Joanna held an impressive position by any account. Yet she did not value status over service to Christ.

---

5   See "Saint Joanna the Myrrhbearer," https://www.oca.org/saints/lives.

FOR REFLECTION

- Joanna seems to have come from a prominent family and certainly was married to a prominent member of Herod's staff. Her people were both the elite of Judea and of the Roman leadership in the area. Does that make it easier or more difficult for her to follow Christ?

- What is the purpose of obtaining John's head? What would have happened to it if Joanna had not retrieved it?

- When has God unexpectedly offered an opportunity for you to help honor someone? Do you think you sometimes miss opportunities for service? Why?

MARY AND MARTHA
OF BETHANY

Among those who ministered to our Lord, two of the most beloved are the sisters of Lazarus, Mary and Martha. While they are not expressly named among the women at Christ's Tomb, Tradition has always counted them among the myrrhbearers and honors them with the others. Nearly everything we know about the sisters comes directly from the scriptural accounts of their interactions with Jesus: We know that they hosted Him for dinner with some frequency and, of course, that He raised their beloved brother, Lazarus, from the dead (Luke 10:38–42; John 11:1–44; 12:1–11).

In an unusually intimate and domestic scene, St. Luke tells the very relatable story of Mary and Martha's quarrels over hosting Jesus for supper: While Mary "sat at Jesus' feet and heard His word," her sister Martha "was distracted with much serving," and, frustrated with her sister, she complained to Jesus, "Lord, do You not care that my sister has left me to serve alone? Therefore tell her to help me" (Luke 10:39–40). Anyone who cooks for dinner parties with beloved guests is familiar with this struggle; dinner must be served and work must be done, but the truly desirable thing is to spend quality time with our guests. It is a challenge to do both—and how much more challenging to see your sister sitting and enjoying the companionship while you do all the work!

The universality of this quarrel and the intimacy of this scene make us feel that we know the sisters well, and many women identify with them, judging their own actions as being like Mary or like Martha. In our American economy, where we express our love by purchasing related merchandise, T-shirts and dish towels are available that say, "Love like Mary, serve like Martha" or "Be Mary in a Martha World" or "More Mary, Less Martha." The sisters have come to symbolize women's spiritual refreshment, their work obligations, and the struggle to balance the two.

Biographical Details

We may feel that we know Mary and Martha well because the Scriptures offer scenes from inside their home and even inside their grief at the death of their brother, but we don't have much biographical data on either of these women outside of these domestic scenes. For instance, we don't know if either sister ever married, though there are curious discrepancies in the identification of the house where they hosted Jesus. The house is mentioned in each of the four Gospels. First, in the tenth chapter of Luke's Gospel, "a certain woman named Martha welcomed Him into her house" (v. 38), where Jesus enjoyed a meal while Martha served and Mary sat at His feet. In John's Gospel, when Jesus comes to raise Lazarus from the dead, the house is simply the home of Lazarus, Mary, and Martha, and John takes care to note that "it was *that* Mary who anointed the Lord with fragrant oil" (John 11:2). Again when he describes the anointing, the house is certainly the home of Lazarus, Mary, and Martha.

But in both the Gospels of Matthew and Mark, Jesus is anointed in Bethany by a woman with an alabaster jar of expensive nard, and the house is explicitly identified as the home of Simon the Leper (see Matt. 26:6–13; Mark 14:3–9). The scenes are very similar, and it seems that all of them are describing Mary, in her home, anointing Christ before His death. Does this mean that the home of Simon the Leper is the same house that Lazarus, Mary, and Martha lived in? If so, then perhaps either Mary or Martha was married to Simon the Leper. He is not mentioned in their lives other than in this detail, so if he did marry one of the sisters, perhaps he had died, and she was now living as a widow. It is also possible that Simon was related to the family in another way, as we do not encounter Mary and Martha as wives or widows, but primarily as Lazarus's sisters.

We do know that Mary and Martha's lives were profoundly changed when Jesus raised their brother from the dead, and not only because this extraordinary miracle happened before their very eyes, and within their own tight-knit family unit. This event attracted no small amount of attention, for St. John tells us that "many of the Jews who had come to Mary, and had seen the things Jesus did, believed in Him" (John 11:45). Word spread to the chief priests and the Pharisees, who saw that their power—their position as the leaders of Israel as recognized by the Roman Empire—was at stake. They began to plot to kill Lazarus as well as Jesus:

> Now a great many of the Jews knew that He was there; and they came, not for Jesus' sake only, but that they might also see Lazarus, whom He had raised from the dead. But the chief priests plotted to put Lazarus to death also, because on account of him many of the Jews went away and believed in Jesus. (John 12:9–11)

As long as he was alive, Lazarus was a literal testament to the saving power of Jesus Christ; he was walking proof of Christ's great miracle. The chief priests plotted to put both Jesus and

Lazarus to death, and after they crucified Jesus, they continued to pursue Lazarus.

Mary and Martha saw how Jesus was persecuted, and they knew well what it meant for those same authorities to come after their brother. This must have been a scary time for them. We do know that Lazarus left Judea, with his sisters at his side—but we don't know for certain whether they were chased out of town in forced exile, or if they simply ran for their lives. They escaped on a ship—it is unclear whether they boarded willingly—and soon the trio found themselves sailing to Cyprus. We do not know much about their early years on Cyprus, but just a few years later, in the year AD 45, they would be visited on the island by the Apostles Paul and Barnabas. The apostles faced strong opposition from the Jewish community there (Acts 13:4–6), and we can infer that perhaps this same group of people were unwelcoming to Mary, Martha, and Lazarus.

But with the visit of the Apostles, Cyprus was transformed. In Paphos, Paul would accomplish miracles, and Luke tells us that "the proconsul believed, when he saw what had been done, being astonished at the teaching of the Lord" (Acts 13:12). This proconsul was likely the first Roman authority to believe in Christ, and in Cyprus Christianity began to grow largely unopposed. The Church there grew quickly, and Paul and Barnabas entrusted the new communities to Lazarus, naming him the first bishop of Kition.

Lazarus's Burden

Lazarus presided over the Church in Cyprus for thirty years, preaching God's word and converting many pagans to Christianity. Mary and Martha were there with him and continued to support and care for him. We don't know if they had a gift for preaching, but their experiences with Jesus and the stories they could tell were likely of great interest to the local population.

Mary and Martha surely were grateful to have their brother back, but Lazarus was profoundly changed by his experience in Hades. According to Tradition, Lazarus stopped smiling after his resurrection. The unredeemed souls and the darkness he had seen in Hades were always on his mind, giving him a somber countenance. Imagine the weight he carried on his shoulders, having spent four days in Hades, and having been chased out of his home lest his own people become his murderers. The responsibilities of a bishop in the early Church under Roman persecution were heavy, as he and his beloved flock faced the very real possibility of martyrdom. Mary and Martha joined him in this burden and supported him.

It is said that Lazarus was seen to laugh only one time after his resurrection: He saw a storekeeper chasing down a young man who had stolen a ceramic pot of some kind, and Lazarus began to chuckle, saying, "The clay steals the clay!"[1] The Bishop of Kition could laugh at the silliness of human beings as we fight over material objects, forgetting that we are made by God and that these possessions have no real importance at all.

We don't know how the lives of these siblings ended, but all three names appear on some ancient lists of martyrs. It's likely that they were martyred for the Faith around AD 75. Mary and Martha offered up everything they had during years of loving service to our Lord, and at the end, they offered up their very lives, earning crowns of martyrdom.

Because Lazarus was the first bishop of Kition, a beautiful marble tomb was built for him in a place of honor inside the church

---

1   M. G. Michaelides, "St. Lazarus, the Friend of Christ and First Bishop of Kition, Cyprus," (1984; repr., Fr. Demetrios Serfes, 2009).

building there. When it was discovered in 890, the inscription read, "Lazarus of the Four Days, the friend of Christ." How beautiful to really be a friend of Jesus, someone He especially loved as He walked this earth! Mary and Martha's graves were not found near Lazarus's tomb, and it's likely that his sisters were buried nearby in a regular cemetery, with the rest of the faithful people of Cyprus.

FOR REFLECTION

- Have you known anyone who was near death, but survived? Has the gratitude and relief you experienced ever worn off?

- Do you think the sisters' gratitude spurred their ongoing service to their brother?

- The raising of Lazarus is a cause for celebration, but one gets the sense that Lazarus did not spend much of his new life celebrating. What do you imagine was on his mind? What did he find in Hades that made him so serious on earth?

NICODEMUS

Nicodemus was a Pharisee, a ruler of the Jews, a man with significant status and power (John 3:1). And yet, in the dark of night, he was teetering toward losing it all. The council was up in arms because Jesus had entered the temple, and finding it full of "money changers doing business," He "drove them all out of the temple," overturning tables and dramatically calling out their lack of reverence and respect (John 2:14–15). This miracle-working Teacher was challenging Jewish leadership and, like so many of God's prophets before Him, exposing the corruption and the rot within. He directly attacked their authority, but Nicodemus didn't react like everyone else. He didn't feel defensive, and he didn't want retribution. He was considering the situation: Maybe Jesus had a point.

That night, Nicodemus found himself walking toward Jesus in the dark. The Teacher was there, sitting with His disciples, in quiet conversation. Nicodemus held back for a moment, still under cover of darkness, considering walking into the soft light. He was torn. How many prophets had God sent to tell the Israelites that they were on the wrong path, that they weren't living up to their part of the covenant? How many prophets had been run out of town? How many had been killed? And yet, Nicodemus was a member of the Sanhedrin, entrusted to protect order. God expected Him to follow His Law and to denounce false teachers. How difficult it is to discern! And yet, there was something powerful and different about this Man, whose words resonated somewhere deep inside Nicodemus. He made a choice. He stepped into the light and looked into the face of Christ.

Out of the Darkness

Nicodemus's words were very clear for a man who still felt conflicted: "Rabbi, we know that You are a teacher come from God; for no one can do these signs that You do unless God is with him" (John 3:2). He spoke as one who knew that Christ was no charlatan.

Jesus' response only served to highlight Nicodemus's struggle: "Most assuredly, I say to you, unless one is born again, he cannot see the kingdom of God" (John 3:3). Nicodemus struggled to comprehend Jesus' words, stuck as he was in the literal and concrete concept of birth. Christ spoke to Him of Spirit and water, and as St. Cyril of Alexandria explains, Nicodemus tried and then failed to understand:

> Nicodemus is convicted hereby of being still carnal, and therefore no way receiving the things of the Spirit of God. For he thinketh that this so dread and illustrious Mystery is foolishness. And hearing of the birth spiritual and from above, he imagineth the carnal womb returning to birth-pang of things already born. . . . The unskilled mind falling upon conceptions of greater calibre than it, being relaxed returns, and ever glad to remain in the measure that suits it, despises an understanding better and loftier than itself. In which case the ruler of the Jews now being, receives not the spiritual birth.[1]

---

1   St. Cyril, Archbishop of Alexandria, *Commentary on the Gospel According to St. John*, bk. 2, sects. 167–68, trans. T. Randall, vol. 7 (James Parker &

Seeing this failure, Jesus challenges him and his suitability to lead Israel directly: "Are you the teacher of Israel, and do not know these things? Most assuredly, I say to you, We speak what We know and testify what We have seen, and you do not receive Our witness. If I have told you earthly things and you do not believe, how will you believe if I tell you heavenly things?" (John 3:10–12).

The most learned, elite men of Israel had neither ears to hear nor eyes to see, and Nicodemus, even though he stood on the cusp of recognizing God in Jesus, was at a loss. He is divided: He wanted to understand and to believe, and yet he was afraid to do so.

Nicodemus appears three times in John's Gospel, and each time he expressly is identified as the one who "came to Jesus by night" (John 3:2; 7:50, 19:39). For John, this is an important, defining quality of Nicodemus. Saint John returns again and again to this theme of Christ as light, contrasted with the darkness of sin and death, and this becomes an important, defining quality of Nicodemus. He is always, even later as he lovingly buries our Lord, the one who came in darkness.

This is the very condition of fallen humanity: Like Nicodemus, we struggle to discern good from bad, light from the darkness. Jesus explains to him,

> The light has come into the world, and men loved darkness rather than light, because their deeds were evil. For everyone practicing evil hates the light and does not come to the light, lest his deeds should be exposed. But he who does the truth comes to the light, that his deeds may be clearly seen, that they have been done in God. (John 3:19–21)

Co., 1874), https://ia801305.us.archive.org/13/items/CyrilOfAlexandria CommentaryOnJohnVolume1Tr.P.E.Pusey1874/cyril.pdf.

Surely Nicodemus felt that resonance in his soul again: God truly was telling them that the high priests and the council, Nicodemus and his companions, were not stewarding God's nation well. Like Nicodemus, they preferred darkness to light, for their hearts and their actions were corrupt. Nicodemus stands at the edge of darkness, but so many of the Jewish leaders remained in deep darkness, lest they be exposed.

Israel's Waning Light

Israel should have been the lamp to shine God's light brightly into the world, a beacon to all the nations. The high priests were to be the stewards of that light, trimming the wick and keeping the oil replenished. In Leviticus, God instructed the Israelites to keep the lamps in the tabernacle burning "from evening until morning before the Lord continually; it shall be an ordinance forever in your generations" (Lev. 24:3).

Israel was called to worship God by keeping its lamps lit "forever"; the lamps were lit every evening for worship—a tradition the Orthodox Church continues in the daily Vespers service, welcoming "the gladsome light of the holy glory."[2] Those lamps were symbols of Israel's love for God: Every evening, the people would kindle that love with worship and praise, and their relationship with God would flourish. But that love and worship cooled, and when Christ came to His people, they did not know Him. When Jesus came to them in the flesh, they rejected Him. The lamp that was Israel rejected the Light of the World and preferred to remain in darkness.

---

2   In the fourth century, Basil the Great would refer to the classic vesperal song, "O Gladsome Light," as an "ancient hymn"; from the beginning, Christians continued this beautiful Jewish tradition of the service of the lighting of the lamps.

As a member of the Sanhedrin, Nicodemus was a leader among the Jews, one of the few expressly responsible for keeping those lamps lit with the light of God—and yet, we know him as the one who came in darkness. Later, Jesus will return for the feast of Tabernacles, and He will preach throughout Jerusalem, sowing division among the Jews as many of them begin to realize that He is the Christ (John 7:41). John writes,

> Then the Pharisees answered them, "Are you also deceived? Have any of the rulers or the Pharisees believed in Him? But this crowd that does not know the law is accursed."
>
> Nicodemus (he who came to Jesus by night, being one of them) said to them, "Does our law judge a man before it hears him and knows what he is doing?"
>
> They answered and said to him, "Are you also from Galilee? Search and look, for no prophet has arisen out of Galilee." And everyone went to his *own* house. (John 7:47–53)

Not Yet Free

When the people began to recognize the Son of God, their leaders answered, "Have any of the rulers or the Pharisees believed in Him?" They remind the people to trust in their teachers, to look to their learned example lest they be deceived. The crowd's recognition of the Savior is quashed by the declaration that none of the rulers or the Pharisees agree with them—and yet, Nicodemus sits right there, a living contradiction of that assertion. He is a ruler and he is a Pharisee, and he believes. He could stand up and say so, but still afraid to risk his status, he simply says, "Does our law judge a man before it hears him?" He knows the Law, and he quietly challenges these hypocrites, who accuse the crowd of ignorance of the Law while they themselves ignore it. He silences them and they go home, leaving Jesus free—but Nicodemus does not choose to lead the people into the light as a teacher of Israel should.

In his commentary on the Gospel of John, St. Cyril of Alexandria said,

> One of the rulers is Nicodemus, and he is numbered among those who had authority, yet not wholly unbelieving nor altogether vying with their folly, but already pricked, not indeed having his love to Christ yet free, yet to some degree feeling shame at the convictions of his conscience. . . . For being still sick of harmful shame, and not yet mingling boldness with his zeal, he permits the faith that is in him to be not seen uncovered, but casting about it dissimulation like a darksome cloak, he as yet conceals that he is on Christ's side; yet is he sick with a grievous sickness.
>
> For we ought to believe fearlessly, glorying rather than ashamed, practising a transparent openness, and refusing slave-befitting dissimulation.[3]

Nicodemus is "pricked"; he feels that Jesus is speaking the truth, and yet he does not come out from the darkness, he does not let the light of his faith shine forth. The high priests of Israel and the Sanhedrin were to be the ones who shone God's light, but by the first century, they had become lampkeepers in name only; they were dark when they should have been filled with light. Caught up in this confusion, Nicodemus and the leaders of Israel struggle

---

3 St. Cyril et al., *Commentary on John*, vol. 1, bk. 5, sect. 558, Ancient Christian Texts (InterVarsity Press, 2013).

with the "grievous sickness" of loving darkness more than light, power more than God.

Unexpected Myrrhbearers

When next we meet Nicodemus, something has changed. Where he once protected his status and position, now he abandons it with reckless faith. When Jesus was first preaching publicly and overturning tables in the temple, it seemed that He might well be the promised King of Israel, come to restore David's throne and to overthrow the Roman occupation. The coming Messiah was understood to bring with Him a new Kingdom, and yet—just as he could not understand how to follow an earthly birth with a spiritual birth—Nicodemus could not trade his earthly power for a seat in the new Kingdom of God.

But Jesus did not lead a rebellion. He did not overthrow the Sanhedrin or attack the Roman Empire.[4] He went gently and quietly like a lamb to the slaughter, He forgave His persecutors as He hung on the Cross, and He died quietly. Nicodemus had known that Jesus truly was sent from God, and that His words were true, but he could not let go of his own safe status. What freed Nicodemus to act so boldly? Was it seeing Christ—whom he really knew in his heart to be the Son of God and Messiah—reject all earthly power and all semblance of might and victory? Did he finally understand that his seat on the council was not a thing

---

4   Christ did, of course, battle and win—He overthrew death, a victory far greater and more formidable than anything Israel imagined. But on the day of His Crucifixion and burial, even His closest followers still had no idea this was His true mission.

worth grasping when compared to the tremendous importance of Christ's presence among us on earth?

Whatever fortified him, when Joseph of Arimathea, also a member of the Sanhedrin and a secret follower of Christ, obtained Christ's body, Nicodemus was at his side. This time, he came in the dying sunlight, trading his political power to serve a Messiah who seemed powerless to give him anything in return.

How could Nicodemus find a way to redeem himself? How could he undo his rejection of Christ and prove his love? By becoming a myrrhbearer:

> And Nicodemus, who at first came to Jesus by night, also came, bringing a mixture of myrrh and aloes, about a hundred pounds. Then they took the body of Jesus, and bound it in strips of linen with the spices. (John 19:39–40)

Nicodemus does not redeem himself with speeches or apologies. He takes action—quiet, simple, practical action. He brings a hundred pounds of myrrh and aloes, those oils of mercy and love, and personally prepares Christ's beaten, bloodied body. In this loving action, he wipes away a lifetime spent in darkness and is reborn to a new life in the light.

Life After the Sanhedrin

Nicodemus brought his faith into the light and was cast out of the synagogue for the rest of his life.[5] He no longer belonged among those who gathered in the darkness. Having lost his home and his influence, he took refuge with Gamaliel, another honorable

---

5   "Finding of the Relics of Righteous Saint Nikódēmos," https://www.oca.org/saints/lives/2014/08/02/102182.

member of the Sanhedrin, who intervened with the council in defense of the apostles: "And now I say to you, keep away from these men and let them alone; for if this plan or this work is of men, it will come to nothing; but if it is of God, you cannot overthrow it—lest you even be found to fight against God" (Acts 5:38-39).

Gamaliel left room for the possibility that Jesus could be "of God," and he also made room for the disgraced Nicodemus in his home in the countryside. Both Gamaliel and Nicodemus are recognized as saints by the Orthodox Church, as they both became Christians. Nicodemus, who had once come to Jesus in the darkness, brought myrrh and aloes in the dying light of Christ's final day on earth, and finished his days as a follower of the Light of the World. When he died peacefully at Gamaliel's home, his friend buried him in a secret grave beside the first martyr, St. Stephen.

FOR REFLECTION

- Nicodemus came at night and kept his faith hidden until Christ was apparently defeated, having died on the Cross. Why do you suppose this was the moment when Nicodemus put his status on the line to serve Christ?

- Are there any areas of your life where fear causes you to hide your faith? Are there times when you want to hide in the darkness?

- Like Israel, you and I were created to serve as lamps. We are meant to be filled with the Light of Christ, illuminating the world. It is easy to say that Israel should have stayed faithful to God, shining brightly with His light. But is it actually easy for us to keep ourselves pure, to hold fast to God in every choice we make, all day long? Can you think of ways to shine more brightly with Christ's love?

JOSEPH OF ARIMATHEA

Nicodemus assisted with Christ's burial, but it was Joseph of Arimathea who bravely approached Pontius Pilate to request His body. In his Gospel, St. Mark, who is usually so terse, describes the scene beautifully:

> Joseph of Arimathea, a prominent council member, who was himself waiting for the kingdom of God, coming and taking courage, went in to Pilate and asked for the body of Jesus. Pilate marveled that He was already dead; and summoning the centurion, he asked him if He had been dead for some time. So when he found out from the centurion, he granted the body to Joseph. Then he bought fine linen, took Him down, and wrapped Him in the linen. And he laid Him in a tomb which had been hewn out of the rock, and rolled a stone against the door of the tomb. (Mark 15:43–46)

Because Joseph was a "prominent council member" and a wealthy man, he had access to Pontius Pilate. Of course, that also means that Joseph had every reason to distance himself from Christ. As Blessed Theophylact writes,

> While yet a servant of the law, the blessed Joseph recognized Christ as God, and this is why he dared to do such a praiseworthy

65

deed of courage. He did not stop to think to himself, "I am a wealthy man, and I will lose my wealth if I ask for the body of one condemned by the rulers authority, and I will be slandered by the Jews." No such thoughts did he harbor, but placing all other considerations second, he begged to bury the Body of the One condemned.[1]

Like so many others, he must have been heartbroken at Jesus' death and apparent defeat. Only love could have compelled Joseph to risk his earthly power, with nothing promised to him in return. All of Jesus' disciples had scattered, but Joseph served our Lord, receiving, preparing, and burying His body despite the dangers he faced.

After the Resurrection

The Gospel of Nicodemus (also called the Acts of Pilate), written in the fourth or fifth century, records a legend about Joseph of Arimathea. Of course, while such books are called "gospels," they aren't Scripture. Many of them seem to be fictional accounts that fill in the biographical details that pious audiences craved. According to that text, even though Joseph obtained permission to bury Jesus, he was imprisoned after the burial, and our risen Lord appeared to him in prison and released him. In an alternate version of the story, Joseph was thrown into a pit and miraculously saved.

Whether or not these details of his life are true, we do know that after Christ's Ascension, Joseph began to live openly as a Christian. He ultimately was banished from Jerusalem—a curse

---

1   Bl. Theophylact, "On Mark 15," in *The Explanation of the Holy Gospel According to St. Mark*, Bl. Theophylact's Explanation of the New Testament, vol. 1 (St. Herman of Alaska Brotherhood/Chrysostom Press, 1992).

that turned out to be a blessing, as this became his opportunity to serve as an apostle. He traveled the world, spreading the gospel of Jesus Christ. The Apostle Philip may have tasked Joseph with leading twelve followers to the distant British Isles, where he preached the Word, establishing churches. According to Tradition, he was buried with dignity and great honor at Glastonbury, England.

FOR REFLECTION

- Joseph offered up his status and position, and he offered his own tomb to Jesus. What did he expect in return? What did he receive?

- Joseph's tomb became the Holy Sepulcher, the location of Christ's Resurrection and surely the most important location for Christian pilgrimage. This is a profound illustration: When we offer up those dead parts of ourselves to the Lord, He transforms them into something beautiful, bursting with life. Joseph offered a tomb, and Christ turned it into the ultimate locus of abundant life. When have you found that God transformed something for you, bringing life from death?

- What difficulty in your life needs God's touch now, to come and bring life to it? What is the first step to making that happen?

Part Two

TRACING THE MYRRHBEARERS' JOURNEY IN THE GOSPELS

OUR HEAVENLY
MYRRHBEARER

As we have seen, the myrrhbearers do not suddenly appear on the scene at Christ's death. They were present with Him long before the Crucifixion and remained part of the early Church community long after. As we trace their stories through the Gospels, we will consider the deeper meaning of bearing myrrh. Naturally, we will identify with the women, seeing ourselves as potential myrrhbearers, sent into the world to serve Christ by serving others. And we are. But isn't it also true that we are the ones who lie dead in a tomb, the ones who suffer and struggle and cannot raise ourselves?

In his Letter to the Romans, St. Paul writes, "Therefore we were buried with Him through baptism into death, that just as Christ was raised from the dead by the glory of the Father, even so we also should walk in newness of life" (6:4).

We are buried with Christ through baptism into death. Three times we descend into the water, drowning the old man and emerging as a new person, filled with new life. And after the baptism, after we have entered into His death, Christ comes to us bearing myrrh: He anoints us with sweet-smelling oil. He chrismates us, sealing the Holy Spirit, the Spirit of Life, inside us.

Jesus sends ministers to us through His Body the Church; He nourishes and transforms us with His Body the Eucharist, and He heals us by pouring down His great mercy. He always is ministering to us. He is our Heavenly Physician who comes to cure us, who transforms our simple biological life into something much larger. We are born of the Spirit into another life, one which has no end. He is our Myrrhbearer, tending to our wounds, feeding us, and healing us.

We begin as individuals who protect ourselves, who cling to our own lives. Ultimately, when we die to ourselves, we become ready to love like Christ loves, ready to die for others. We die and become willing to die, learning to stop grasping at life—only to find that in doing so, we enter into life more abundant than we ever imagined. We find ourselves a part of a larger network of people, sharing one another's burdens and living in the Kingdom right here on earth, with our loving, myrrhbearing Lord nourishing and caring for us. What a blessing it is to enter into death with Him, and to come out the other side into abundant life!

As we work our way through the scriptural accounts of the Holy Myrrhbearers, let us be alert to the ways in which Christ has given new life to these individual women and how, through their loving response and merciful service, they find themselves entering ever more deeply into communion with God and one another. As St. John declares, "We love Him because He first loved us," and indeed, we become His myrrhbearers because He first bore myrrh for us (1 John 4:19).

FOR REFLECTION

- It is a classic paradox of Christian life: We must lose our lives to gain true life. What has that meant for you?

- Dying to ourselves means putting aside our own will and embracing God's will for us. In what ways are you ready to stop grasping at something in your life? In what ways are you not ready to give it up?

- When we pray for our enemies and for the entire world, we train our hearts to grow into loving everyone, not just those close to us. Loving our enemies is a kind of death to ourselves and our own self-interest, and so it is a necessary step on our path as Christians. Are there enemies for whom you struggle to pray or anyone for whom you cannot ask God's mercy and compassion? Why?

THE UNNAMED
MYRRHBEARING WOMAN

After His Baptism, Jesus "returned in the power of the Spirit to Galilee" (Luke 4:14–15), casting out demons and healing diseases of every kind, all culminating in the climactic resurrection of a widow's only son. After this very beautiful and impressive beginning to His ministry, it was time to move beyond Galilee. Just before leaving, He encountered an unnamed repentant woman bearing myrrh:

> And behold, a woman in the city who was a sinner, when she knew that *Jesus* sat at the table in the Pharisee's house, brought an alabaster flask of fragrant oil, and stood at His feet behind *Him* weeping; and she began to wash His feet with her tears, and wiped *them* with the hair of her head; and she kissed His feet and anointed them with the fragrant oil. (Luke 7:37–38)

Eyes of Repentance

In Galilee, a profoundly repentant woman anoints Jesus for the ministry ahead with a loving and intimate gesture. Her tears flowed so profusely that she washed His feet with them—God granted her the gift of the tears, and she used her gift to humbly serve our Lord.

The Pharisee was unrepentant; in his pride, he was unaware of his own sins. The woman, on the other hand, knew herself, because in her humility she was perfectly honest with herself. The Pharisee had no idea that he was blinded by his self-righteousness, but she knew she was a sinner, and she knew that Jesus was Lord. Confident in his own virtues, the Pharisee assumed that if Jesus were holy, He would shrink from this woman's touch—but to the contrary, Jesus welcomed both her repentance and her offering:

> Do you see this woman? I entered your house; you gave Me no water for My feet, but she has washed My feet with her tears and wiped *them* with the hair of her head. You gave Me no kiss, but this woman has not ceased to kiss My feet since the time I came in. You did not anoint My head with oil, but this woman has anointed My feet with fragrant oil. Therefore I say to you, her sins, *which are* many, are forgiven, for she loved much. But to whom little is forgiven, *the same* loves little. (Luke 7:44–47)

The Pharisee loved little, but this woman's love ran deep; her love was made manifest in physical action. Her sins were forgiven, and she was reconciled to the Lord and brought into the Kingdom.

In a beautiful sermon about this repentant woman, Peter Chrysologus, the fifth-century bishop of Ravenna, looks to her as an example to us all:

> With her hands of good works, she holds the feet of those who preach His Kingdom. She washes them with tears of charity, kisses them with praising lips and pours out the whole ointment of mercy, until He will turn to her. This means that He will come back to her and say to Simon, to the Pharisees, to those who deny, to the nation of the Jews, "I came into your house. You gave me no water for my feet."

When will He speak these words? He will speak them when He will come in the Majesty of His Father and separate the righteous from the unrighteous, like a shepherd who separates the sheep from the goats. He will say, "I was hungry and you did not give me to eat. I was thirsty and you gave me no drink. I was a stranger and you did not take me in." This is equivalent to saying, "But this woman, while she was bathing my feet, anointing them and kissing them, did to the servants what you did not do for the Master." She did for the feet, what you refused to the Head. She expended upon the lowliest members, what you refused to your Creator. Then He will say to the Church, "Your sins, many as they are, are forgiven you because you have loved much."[1]

This woman extended upon Jesus' lowly feet the honor due the Creator: "As you did *it* to one of the least of these My brethren, you did *it* to Me" (Matt. 25:40). She will be welcomed into the Kingdom for her concrete and loving response to Christ.

The Myrrhbearing Woman Is the Church

This first myrrhbearing woman points to a reality beyond herself. In the same sermon, Peter Chrysologus also said, "Who is this woman? Beyond any doubt, she is the church." Beyond any doubt, *she is the Church*—she is all of us. We are all called to a repentance like hers; God asks us to look honestly at ourselves, without pride to blind us, that we might see our sins and bring them to our Lord, with tearful contrition. And like her, we are called to honor and to serve one another, to minister to the bodies of those around us.

---

1   Ignatius Smith, "St. Peter Chrysologus," Sermon 95, *The Catholic Encyclopedia*, vol. 11 (Robert Appleton Company, 1911), https://www.newadvent.org/cathen/11762c.htm.

As the Pharisees questioned Jesus' authority to forgive sins, Luke tells us that Jesus said to this woman, "Your faith has saved you. Go in peace" (Luke 7:50). Although she had arrived in turmoil, crying over her sins, she left the Pharisee's house with tranquility. Having transformed her tears, Jesus now transformed her heart, granting her great peace.

This woman's repentance and her love for Christ are so great that the tears pour out of her; they mingle with the myrrh, becoming myrrh. God is like that. Everything He touches takes on new life, new significance. He transforms her pain and compunction into a sweet-smelling myrrh of great value, worthy to honor the King. When we offer up our hearts, our tears, He will transform them too.

FOR REFLECTION

• It is often said that the holier a person becomes, the more aware they are of small sins that the rest of us would not even recognize as sinful. If this is the case, is it ever possible *not* to be blind to at least some of our own sins as the Pharisee is?

• As this woman offers up her repentance to Christ, she becomes a model of confession: Truly repentant, she holds nothing back, but rushes into Jesus' presence with trust, humility, and love. How often do we allow ourselves to sink into our sins, preferring darkness to the light of His forgiveness? How often do we come to confession, reluctant to name our sins, hiding our disease from Christ instead of running to our Heavenly Physician for healing?

• How can real repentance help us become a force of love in this world? How might awareness of our own sinfulness and unworthiness help us to find compassion for our neighbor?

THE WOMEN DISCIPLES

The population of Galilee, where Jesus grew up, was not as uniformly Jewish as other areas of Judea. Many Gentiles lived in this area, worshipping Greek and Roman gods. At the time of the Maccabees, in the centuries just before Christ was born, many of the Gentiles in Galilee converted to Judaism, but they were generally considered less Jewish than the "real" Jews of Judea. They were considered second class because they were more influenced by Greek culture, than by the purer culture of Judea.[1]

Matthew tells us that Christ's journeys there fulfilled Isaiah's prophecy:

By the way of the sea, beyond the Jordan,
Galilee of the Gentiles:
The people who sat in darkness have seen a great light,
and upon those who sat in the region and shadow of death
Light has dawned. (Matt. 4:15–16)

Saint John Chrysostom expounds on this vision of Galilee as a darkened place:

---

1 The situation was not unlike that of the Samaritans, who believed in the Jewish God, but were not considered fellow Jews. For more on Galilee of the Gentiles, see the footnote for Matthew 4:15 in the Orthodox Study Bible.

The light of itself sprang up and shone forth: it was not that they first ran to the light. For in truth the condition of men was at the worst before Christ's coming. Since they more than "walked in darkness;" they "sat in darkness;" a kind of sign that they did not even hope to be delivered. For as persons not even knowing where to put a step forward, so they sat, overtaken by the darkness, not being able so much as to stand any more.[2]

The people of Galilee were in a terrible condition—stuck, sitting in the darkness. It seems that they were even beyond repentance, which requires movement, a change of direction. Lost in the dark, they could not even know where to step or how to turn. And at that darkest moment, the Light dawned in Galilee.

The Light Himself brought the glad tidings of the Kingdom of God into the darkness. The Son of God took flesh, and when the time was right, He began His public ministry in the region where He'd grown up. The Gospel of Luke tells us in the eighth chapter that Jesus traveled "through every city and village, preaching and bringing the glad tidings of the kingdom of God." With Him were the twelve disciples and "certain women who had been healed of evil spirits and infirmities," including the women we've already encountered—Mary Magdalene, Joanna the wife of Herod's steward Chuza, and Susanna. Other unnamed followers also "provided for Him from their substance" (vv. 1–3).

Be Filled

As we have discussed, Jesus had expelled seven demons from Mary Magdalene. But her continued healing, and the healing of the

---

2   Chrysostom, "Homily 14" on Matthew, https://www.newadvent.org/fathers/200114.htm

others, required ongoing cooperation with God. Jesus warned in his teachings that an exorcised demon can come back:

When an unclean spirit goes out of a man, he goes through dry places, seeking rest, and finds none. Then he says, "I will return to my house from which I came." And when he comes, he finds *it* empty, swept, and put in order. Then he goes and takes with him seven other spirits more wicked than himself, and they enter and dwell there; and the last *state* of that man is worse than the first. (Matt. 12:43–45)

Once the spirits were cast out, the cleansed person had to find a way to be filled, lest they remain an empty shell, clean and ready to host even more demons. Jesus had freed her, but Mary Magdalene still had work to do: She would have to repent, turning toward Christ. Mary had to become filled with the love of God so that there would be no room for the spirits that had overtaken her. As Elder Thaddeus notes, "where there is prayer, the fallen spirits have no power."[3] When we are filled with love for God, with joy and hope, there is no room for any demonic power to find its way in.

We don't know the details of Jesus' various encounters with the Galilean women, but He healed each of them in a profound way. We read in the Gospels that the twelve disciples left everything to follow Jesus (Matt. 19:27). We are not given the details of what these women left behind, but we can see that, having been freed from the powers of darkness and infirmity, they gave themselves to Him. All the disciples, male and female, died to themselves in some way in order to take this journey—they left their people and

---

3   Elder Thaddeus of Vitovnica, *Our Thoughts Determine Our Lives: The Life and Teachings of Elder Thaddeus of Vitovnica*, trans. Ana Smiljanic (St. Herman of Alaska Brotherhood, 2009).

plans, comfortable homes and secure livings, without knowing what awaited them. And so Jesus headed out of Galilee with the Twelve, and also with the women and "many others" who traveled with Him.

Greater than All Miracles

These women were with Jesus and His disciples all along, traveling with them. But unlike the disciples, these myrrhbearing women remained with Him all the way to the end. Mark tells us that when Jesus was on the Cross, women were "looking on from afar": Mary Magdalene, Mary the mother of James the Less and Joses,[4] and Salome, "who also followed Him and ministered to Him when He was in Galilee, and many other women who came up with Him to Jerusalem" (Mark 15:40–41).

The women He healed in Galilee never wavered and never scattered. They dedicated their fortunes to Him in every sense of the word, both by giving their funds to provide for Him and by tying their very destinies to Christ's. In one of his sermons, St. John Chrysostom says,

> For women, it is said, followed Him and ministered unto Him. . . . For almsgiving is the mother of love, of that love, which is the characteristic of Christianity, which is greater than all miracles, by which the disciples of Christ are manifested. It is the medicine of our sins, the cleansing of the filth of our souls, the ladder fixed to heaven; it binds together the body of Christ.[5]

---

4   That is, of course, Mary the wife of Clopas.
5   St. John Chrysostom, "Homily 6 on Titus," trans. Philip Schaff, in *Nicene and Post-Nicene Fathers, First Series*, vol. 13, rev. ed., ed. Kevin Knight (New Advent), https://www.newadvent.org/fathers/23086.htm.

The women's almsgiving was "something greater than all miracles": the opportunity to live out their love by providing for Jesus "from their substance." Their almsgiving became medicine for their sins, cleansing their souls. The miracles Jesus performed simply set the women free to make a change, lighting the way so that they could see the holy path before them. Once they were reborn as new women, it was up to them to follow that path, and through service to others, they grew and were sanctified.

So often, when we consider Christ's call to serve one another, to feed the hungry and visit the sick, we assume that His goal is simply the care of the downtrodden. In fact, He is not only building up the weak among us; He is at work on our hearts. Loving service is the medicine that will heal our souls and wash away our sins. This is our opportunity to become the Body of Christ, doing His work and becoming truly integrated into the communion that is His holy Church.

FOR REFLECTION

- Theophylact of Ochrid said, "The light has dawned on us, for we were not seeking it, but it appeared to us as if it were pursuing us."[6] The people of Galilee did not know to seek the light or even to hope for it, but the Light pursued them. In your own life, can you see where God has pursued you? Do you expect God to pursue you in the future?

- When the women and the disciples dropped everything and followed Jesus, they very literally walked away from their old lives to begin a new life in Christ. In what ways have you left your old life behind to embrace a new life in Christ?

- Saint John Chrysostom called almsgiving "the medicine of our sins." Have you experienced spiritual healing through almsgiving, perhaps by serving others or through faithful financial stewardship?

---

6   Bl. Theophylact , "On Matthew 4," in *The Explanation of the Holy Gospel*.

THE HOSTESS

M ary and Martha of Bethany, the sisters of Lazarus, are listed
among the eight known myrrhbearing women, though the
Gospels do not specifically name them at the Tomb. They were
certainly members of the inner circle of Christ's followers, and
they may well have been at the Tomb. But perhaps the Church
includes them in the list because they ministered to our Lord long
before His arrest and Crucifixion.

Lazarus's sisters appear in the Gospels three times: First, Luke
describes a meal in their home; then John relates their interactions
with Christ around Lazarus's death and resurrection; and finally,
John describes another meal in their home. Mary and Martha are
featured more in the Gospels than any of the other myrrhbearing
women—except for Mary, the Mother of God.

Distraction and Division

Chronologically, the earliest mention of the sisters comes in Luke's
Gospel, when Martha welcomes Jesus and His disciples into the
family's home. This passage is well-known and is especially well-
loved by those female readers of Scripture who may have been
taught that their primary role is to cook and to take care of the
home. At Lazarus's house, Jesus weighs in directly, declaring that
a woman's spiritual life takes precedence over housework.

87

Now it happened as they went that He entered a certain village; and a certain woman named Martha welcomed Him into her house. And she had a sister called Mary, who also sat at Jesus' feet and heard His word. But Martha was distracted with much serving, and she approached Him and said, "Lord, do You not care that my sister has left me to serve alone? Therefore tell her to help me."

And Jesus answered and said to her, "Martha, Martha, you are worried and troubled about many things. But one thing is needed, and Mary has chosen that good part, which will not be taken away from her." (Luke 10:38–42)

Of course, this lesson also applies to men—to all Christians. We are all called to literal, physical service, feeding and clothing and caring for each other. At the same time, we also are called to prayer and spiritual contemplation. In this brief domestic scene, the service that the myrrhbearing women provided for Jesus and His disciples is fleshed out: We catch a glimpse of hospitality and gain some insight into what it might be like to host God in one's home. Surely Martha was intent on serving her honored guest well, but as is so often the case when we host important people, she succumbed to hurry and stress.

We all know that tension: We want our guests to feel welcomed and loved, but the pressure of completing all the necessary tasks on time begins to build. Like Martha we grow "worried and troubled about many things," rushing to make sure that each guest is served and that all the various foods are ready at the same moment. We feel like we don't have enough hands or time or brain cells to make it all happen as we'd planned. It is noteworthy that Martha is distracted about many things: Instead of being focused, her attention is divided and confused. Mary, on the other hand, is focused on one thing. There is a unity to Mary's mind that Martha has lost. We have all been in Martha's shoes: When the plan doesn't come together as smoothly as we'd hoped, we often lose sight of the real goal of our hospitality. We are no longer single-mindedly pursuing the care and feeding of our guests, but instead our minds are divided and moving frenetically from one thought to another.

If these details and activities are *distracting* Martha, we might ask, distracting her from what? If her job is to serve the guests, we can be sure that she's not distracted from her work. Instead, she is distracted from the one needed thing, the "good part" that Mary has chosen: to spend time with Jesus and listen to Him along with the other disciples. Mary's posture, sitting at her Lord's feet, is a beautiful combination of physical rest and spiritual contemplation. She is not fussing and busy like her sister; she is focused and calm. She is not sleeping or lazy; she is actively listening, taking in Jesus' words. She is *still*. The good part that Mary chose is like those moments that we set aside to spend in prayer: We embrace stillness and manage to be at rest while also being actively engaged, reaching out for connection with God and listening for His word.

An Icon of the Kingdom

Christ refused to send Mary into the kitchen to work. What does that mean? According to Blessed Theophylact,

> Hospitality, which Martha displays, is a great virtue which ought not to be scorned; but it is even greater to give heed to spiritual words. By means of the first, the body is nourished; by means of the second, the soul is brought to life. [...] He did not say anything to Martha until she had first given Him a reason to rebuke her. Only when she tried to draw her sister away from listening

did the Lord take the occasion to rebuke her. To practice hospitality is honorable, until that point is reached when it causes turmoil and draws us away from the things that are more important. [...] it is not hospitality which the Lord forbids, but the extravagance and upset, that is, distractions and turmoil. Simple hospitality He praises.[1]

Theophylact's point is important: Our Lord didn't disparage hospitality—let alone physically ministering to one another—and He did not even spontaneously remark on Martha's hurry. He didn't speak up to criticize her. It was only when Martha asked Jesus to deny Mary's access to Him that He reproved Martha. Had she kept her concerns to herself, He might never have spoken on the topic at all.

There can be no meals without the effort necessary to prepare them and clean up afterward. Work is necessary—especially these fundamental, life-sustaining practices that nourish bodies and keep homes. At the same time, not all work is necessary. We often make our lives more complicated than they need to be and our days busier than they should be. But whether the work we do is necessary or important, or self-imposed and unnecessarily stressful, Jesus teaches us that we must take rest in Him.

We know that "God blessed the seventh day and sanctified it" (Gen. 2:3). He made rest itself holy. Saint Ephrem the Syrian explains,

It was not because he rested on that day that God, who does not weary, blessed and sanctified the seventh day. Nor was it because he was to give it to that people, who did not understand that since

---

1   Bl. Theophylact, *The Explanation of the Holy Gospel According to Luke.*

they were freed from their servitude, they were to give rest to their servants and maidservants. . . . It was given to them in order to depict by a temporal rest, which he gave to a temporal people, the mystery of the true rest, which will be given to the eternal people in the eternal world.[2]

God knows that we need rest and that we might otherwise work ourselves into oblivion. But what He gives us is something more than just physical rest: Rest is an icon of the Kingdom. He gives us a glimpse of the Kingdom of God, a foretaste of the true rest to come, when Christ returns to rule a new heaven and a new earth.

Sitting at Christ's feet, Mary enjoyed a kind of spiritual rest, a communion with our Lord that is active, not passive; she was growing and learning and becoming ever more devoted to Him. Perhaps as we grow in our spiritual lives, we can find a way to be at His feet even when we are at work, serving the people He created. Rather than allowing our minds to become divided and distracted, we can cultivate an interior peacefulness. St. Paul instructs us to "rejoice always, pray without ceasing, [and] in everything give thanks; for this is the will of God in Christ Jesus for you" (1 Thess. 5:16–18). If we can find a way to keep our focus on Christ, as Mary's was, we will find that our hearts remain peaceful as we go about our daily tasks. This is true rest, a glimpse of the Kingdom, and it is always within our grasp.

---

2   St. Ephrem the Syrian, "Commentary on Genesis" I.32–33, in *St. Ephrem the Syrian Selected Prose Works: Commentary on Genesis, Commentary on Exodus, Homily on Our Lord, and Letter to Publius,* The Fathers of the Church Patristic Series (Catholic University of America Press, 1994), 424.

FOR REFLECTION

- What distracts you from focusing on Christ?

- How do you find rest in the midst of your own busyness?

- Could you benefit from a more intentional plan to seek spiritual connection with God?

SAVED IN COMMUNITY

Let's take a closer look at Martha's actions. When Jesus came to her home for a meal, and Mary took her place at His feet, Martha was not only distracted and busy—she was also frustrated and angry with her sister. Unable to focus on the joy of breaking bread with the beloved people around her, Martha asked Jesus to intervene and "tell her to help me." Had Jesus agreed to Martha's request, Mary would have been rebuked for her devotion to our Lord and sent back to the kitchen to work. Instead, He took Mary's side and refused to give Martha what she wanted.

What exactly was the problem with Martha's behavior? She was hosting our Lord and wanted to do a good job of it, but her hurry and anxiety were getting in the way. Her frame of mind was all wrong. Jesus was teaching in the next room, but Martha didn't hear a word. She was preoccupied with many things, probably including her inner monologue about her sister. (I can easily imagine it because I've been there.) Surely a voice in her head complained that Mary had abandoned her. Perhaps she envied Mary's position at our Lord's feet, or maybe her complaints had evolved into accusations that her sister always had been lazy. In my own experience, I have found that both are true: Envy and frustration grow into judgment and resentment. The enemy whispered into Martha's ear, whipping up her self-righteousness, pitting her against her faithful sister, and causing her to interrupt our Lord's teaching with complaints and demands. Yet even keeping silence while harboring such resentment can affect family life, as Elder Thaddeus notes:

> In a large family it is enough for one person to be dissatisfied. The person need not show it—it is sufficient if he begins to breed thoughts of self-pity, of how he is mistreated by his neighbors— and the peace in that family is disturbed. A person can disturb the peace of the whole family with his thoughts. Then everyone is unhappy and no one knows the reason why.[1]

Healing Interactions

Offering hospitality is more than simply providing a meal: It means inviting a guest into our home and nourishing them physically with food and also spiritually with love and connection. Hospitality brings us into communion with one another, but Martha was missing that very love and connection she hoped to provide. She began to see dinner as a list of food preparation tasks instead of appreciating the meal as a love offering. We always are meant to be drawing into communion with one another, with the Holy Trinity as our quintessential example: three Persons in perfect oneness. Jesus prays that His followers would be one just as the Holy Trinity is one, and yet here we see two of His followers, sisters in Christ and in biological reality, at odds with one another.

Martha and Mary were not engaged in a bitter feud; they simply experienced the kind of everyday irritation that marks each of our lives. But this sort of small struggle is the stuff of our salvation. It's hard enough not to judge a faraway enemy, but how much more difficult is it to get along with our siblings? We can pray for hungry people across the globe and hope for world peace.

---

1   Elder Thaddeus of Vitovnica, 194.

The harder thing is to develop the humility necessary to endure the little irritations caused by those real people in our own houses. A quotation commonly attributed to Mother Teresa, the beloved twentieth-century Roman Catholic nun, rings true: "It is easy to love the people far away. It is not always easy to love those close to us. It is easier to give a cup of rice to relieve hunger than to relieve the loneliness and pain of someone unloved in our own home. Bring love into your home, for this is where our love for each other must start."

To be patient with the people in our own homes is no small thing; we are healed through these interactions. When we learn to hold our tongue, to be patient, to be humble, to love one another even when it's hard to do, we are becoming better. Like river rocks, we find that our rough edges are rubbed smooth by each other's flaws. In this way, the people in our daily lives play a big part in our salvation. Mother Teresa also is said to have advised, "What can you do to promote world peace? Go home and love your family."[2] Ultimately, world peace—the healing of all humanity—must be built up one household at a time.

Surely Martha began with a hope of offering a loving space to our Lord; she wanted not just to put a meal on the table, but truly to be a myrrhbearer, nourishing her guests physically and emotionally. But her frustration and resentment overtook her. It is so easy to have a commendable goal in mind but to fail spiritually in the execution, as we find ourselves turning into anxious, frustrated, even angry people. The spiritual challenge is to accomplish the good thing in a good way, without stepping on or snapping at anyone along the path—to move through this world together, in communion with one another and with Christ.

---

2   Mother Teresa likely said something like this several times, but unfortunately there's no precise source to cite.

True Abundance

At another point shortly after this moment in Luke's Gospel, another pair of siblings is locked in conflict, again asking Christ to step in and take sides:

> Then one from the crowd said to Him, "Teacher, tell my brother to divide the inheritance with me."
>
> But He said to him, "Man, who made Me a judge or an arbitrator over you?" And He said to them, "Take heed and beware of covetousness, for one's life does not consist in the abundance of the things he possesses." (Luke 12:13–15)

Like Martha, this brother may well have had a reasonable complaint: Things simply weren't *fair*. How often does this cry rise up among siblings? How often are children praying, "Lord, it's not fair! Please fix it." And yet, Jesus refuses to intervene. Keeping things fair doesn't much concern Him. Instead, He peers directly into our hearts and shows us the murky motives and desires hidden there. Whether we receive our fair share of Dad's property, or whether our sister does her fair share of the work, is simply not God's concern. Jesus cares only about the state of our hearts and sees every situation as an opportunity for our hearts to grow.

We will not find life in material abundance or in the fair distribution of resources and effort. True life, eternal life, consists of communion with Christ and with others, and we cannot be in communion so long as we are squabbling and resentful. When we sin—coveting our brother's possessions or judging our sister's behavior—we create disharmony. We interrupt that communion by pulling away.

I once said something about "fairness" to my priest, and he looked up at me, surprised.

"God doesn't care about fairness!" he insisted. "If He did, where would we be? If He gave us what we fairly deserved, no one could ever be saved!" We are not worthy of God's gifts, but instead, we should be grateful that rather than mete out what is fairly deserved, He works for our salvation.

God doesn't offer us fairness. He offers mercy. He doesn't give up on us, but instead He offers us opportunities to grow and to be transformed in Him. He saves us and He forgives us, though we don't deserve it. In the Gospel according to St. John, Jesus says, "I have come that they may have life, and that they may have it more abundantly" (John 10:10). Jesus does not offer fairness or equity; He offers life.

Our lives are full of small interactions with our families and with friends, with people like us and with some who seem very different from us. Each contact is an opportunity to respond to the human being in front of us with love and mercy, or to break away into disharmony and complaints. God extends His love to us and invites us into communion with Him. May we all learn how to hold on to the peace He sends us and how to maintain that communion with Him and with others at all times.

FOR REFLECTION

- Do you find yourself demanding fairness from God?

- What kinds of interactions challenge you most, sending you toward disharmony and complaints? Do you find yourself most easily irritated by family members?

- What can you do differently during those interactions that are most challenging for you?

WAITING ON THE LORD

When we're confronted with the serious illness of a loved one, the smaller questions that usually occupy our minds tend to fade away. We may have spent day after day thinking about the minutia of ordinary life and its work—focused, as it were, on the minutes of our day, and what we will accomplish as they tick by—but when the specter of death appears, our attention moves to eternity. We pull back from our close-up view to see the bigger picture: Life is limited, and time runs out for us. Our loved one may not come to breakfast tomorrow morning, may not appear in the doorway anymore. Even from our Christian perspective, with our hope for eternal life, there is a finality to death: Our existence on earth, as we know it, is finite.

A Shift

When last we considered Martha, she was frustrated with her sister's contemplative stance; the two were at odds, because Mary was not helping in the kitchen. But when the sisters appear in John's Gospel, things have changed, for their brother Lazarus has become terribly sick. The family knew Jesus well; John tells us that "Jesus loved Martha and her sister and Lazarus" (John 11:5). Naturally, as faithful disciples, their first instinct when Lazarus fell ill is to call for Jesus. They send a messenger, an intercessor who could plead on their behalf to our Lord: "Therefore the sisters sent to Him, saying, 'Lord, behold, he whom You love is sick'" (John 11:3). John's words—"the sisters sent"—indicate a joint action. They are no longer at odds but act together to send out the call for Jesus, filled with faith in His ability to heal and confident that, because He loved their brother, He would hurry to come help. And when Jesus finally arrives in Bethany, though they speak to Him at different times, they say the same thing: "Lord, if You had been here, my brother would not have died" (John 11:21, 32). The two women are in perfect accord.

Together, the sisters send for the Lord, and together they nurse their sick brother. No longer hurried and distracted, they dedicate themselves wholeheartedly to their myrrhbearing service: nourishing him, working to alleviate his pain, comforting him. Unlike throwing a dinner party, this is the sort of work we can do more easily at our Lord's feet: When we are connected to Him in prayer, the very care we give to a dying family member becomes a prayer.

Time was passing. The sisters were worried about Lazarus when they sent word to Jesus, and they knew exactly how long it would take the messenger to reach him. Surely they watched and waited—as they nursed their dying brother, they calculated the messenger's path. With every hour, the wait must have grown more agonizing. Even in today's modern world, with all our impressive medical advances, we find ourselves sitting beside our loved ones, powerless. All we can do is lift them before Christ, offer them up to His loving care: "Thy will be done." We wait just as Martha and Mary did, offering love and care, prayer and hope, and watching to see if He will act. They hoped for a miracle, but they also knew that time was running out.

Those waiting times have a strange quality: quiet but not tranquil, still but not peaceful. How many people are waiting, suspended between a loved one's illness and their death, at this very moment? They have nothing to do but pray and wait, to see whether this illness turns around or takes their beloved one forever. Many of us drive past hospitals every day, scarcely thinking about the people inside. Each one has room after room of patients inside, most of whom are surrounded by family members like Mary and Martha. How many parents sit beside their child's bed? How many husbands and wives pray for an intervention that will spare them this loss? How many siblings sit beside their lifelong companion, and hope that Jesus will show Himself soon?

Mary and Martha's prayer, "Lord, the one whom You love is sick," expressed confidence in His love: They did not doubt that Jesus loved them and their brother, and they did not doubt His power to transform this terrible trajectory that Lazarus's fate had taken. Jesus did love them, and He did have this power—and yet, when He heard their prayer, Jesus did not immediately go to them, but very intentionally "stayed two more days" before leaving for Bethany (John 11:6). We may have great faith that our Lord can heal anything, but we also know that He does not always intervene. Sometimes He tarries, and sometimes He allows the suffering to continue, and sometimes we bury the ones we love. All we can do is wait until His will is revealed.

Death's approach reminds us that we are not in control; it puts us in our place. We may spend most of our time thinking that we are taking care of things, paying the bills, making dinner, orchestrating our plans—but when the veil is pulled away, we recall that we were never really in charge of anything. God is pouring gifts down on us, and we—blinded by our pride—believe that we've earned all these blessings. But in the face of death, we are finally honest. We "know this: the Lord, He is God; / He made us, and not we ourselves; / We are His people and the sheep of His pasture" (Ps. 99/100:3). We are God's creatures, and we cannot save ourselves. Only our Shepherd can save us.

When our impotence is obvious, when our loved one sits at the brink of death, we are forced to turn to God because He is the only One who can possibly intervene. We are finally humbled—and that is the moment when God can best work with us. In that humility and quiet, our hearts are soft and bruised . . . and pliable. We stop fighting and allow God to form us into the person He created us to be. This idea is expressed beautifully in the poetic prayer commonly attributed to St. Irenaeus of Lyon:

> It is not you that shapes God,
> It is God that shapes you.
> If you are the work of God,
> await the hand of the artist who does all things in due season.
> Offer him your heart, soft and tractable,
> and keep the form in which the artist has fashioned you.
> Let your clay be moist, lest you grow hard
> and lose the imprint of his fingers.

In those quiet days, Lazarus's sisters sat vigil by his side, pliable, ready to be formed by God. They waited for Jesus to come with His healing powers, and eventually, they waited for Lazarus to breathe his last. Without the distraction and the anxiety, they cared for their sick brother together, doing the work of myrrhbearing and providing love and comfort, their communion restored. Something was healed in them as the world came back into focus: They remembered that we are made by God and cannot save ourselves. Humbled and waiting, they worked together of one accord, and their hearts were softened. They endured these strange days of waiting and working, spending what might be their last hours with their beloved brother, and asking why Jesus had not yet come to spare his life. The sisters offered up humble hearts and loving service, and in response God prepared them for the most extraordinary developments.

FOR REFLECTION

- Those in-between times when we face the unknown can be the most difficult. When were you last in an in-between time?

- When do you find yourself face-to-face with your powerlessness?

- Is there a way to offer yourself up to God in those moments? How can you cooperate with His efforts, becoming pliable and putting yourself in a position to be transformed?

A COMMUNITY GATHERED

Martha and Mary hoped that their message would reach Jesus in time, and that He would hurry to their brother; and yet, as the hours passed, their hope faded. Their brother died. The waiting was over. Many of us know the shocking silence of that time, our numbness and attempts to step forward, working to convince our brains of the new normal we're entering.

This can be a very isolating experience: One beloved person is torn away, and those left behind often feel as if everyone were gone or as if they are separated from others by the fog of grief. In the best circumstances, people come and gather around the grieving ones, offering warm foods and comforting hugs. Nothing they will say or do can fix the terrible loss, but their very presence is a balm. To sit beside a suffering person, enduring the dark places with them, is a great gift. Fellow humans cannot relieve the pain, but we can come together, offering food and love. Indeed, for thousands of years the Jewish people have done just this, observing the very beautiful custom of "sitting shiva": Friends and loved ones gather with the bereaved family immediately after the burial and sit together in their grief for seven days.[1] The tradition is specifically to sit in a low place—chairs may be replaced with stools, or, in the Old Testament, mourners were seated on the ground. Job's

---

1   Joseph and his brothers sat shiva for their father, Jacob (Gen. 50:10).

friends came to "mourn with him, and to comfort him. . . . So they sat down with him on the ground seven days and seven nights, and no one spoke a word to him, for they saw that *his* grief was very great" (Job 2:11, 13 [NKJV]). They come down to his low, miserable level, and they do not speak or try to distract him. They sit with him in his pain, there to listen or to sit in silence. In this way, the community loves its members through their most difficult days.

Company in Grief

Saint John tells us that just such a crowd gathered around these sisters as they grieved. In addition to their local friends and family in Bethany, larger crowds came to Martha and Mary from nearby Jerusalem "to comfort them concerning their brother" (John 11:18–19).

They came not to gawk or gossip, but to offer their presence in the midst of the sisters' grief. The family was likely well loved, and we see that love expressed in this outpouring of support. These friends likely helped the sisters prepare Lazarus's body according to their custom, wrapping him in linens with myrrh and spices. Mary and Martha, ever the myrrhbearers themselves, were part of a larger community who assisted them in their own time of need. The women took care of one another, sitting with the sisters, day after day. And when Mary stood up to leave, "the Jews who were with her in the house, and comforting her, when they saw that Mary rose up quickly and went out, followed her, saying, 'She is going to the tomb to weep there'" (John 11:31). They didn't fall away, but stayed close, to join her in her weeping.

Friends and neighbors were truly there to be *with* Mary, staying close to her side as she worked her way through the pain of this loss. They demonstrated real generosity in the decision to lay aside work and other plans to join the sisters' walk through grief for a time.

John Chrysostom wondered at the idea that even as the high priests were scheming to kill Jesus, so many Jews came out to Bethany to show support for a family that so conspicuously followed Him:

> Two miles. This is mentioned to account for so many coming from Jerusalem: And many of the Jews came to Martha and Mary, to comfort them concerning their brother. But how could the Jews be consoling the beloved of Christ, when they had resolved that whoever confessed Christ should be put out of the synagogue? Perhaps the extreme affliction of the sisters excited their sympathy; or they wished to show respect for their rank. Or perhaps they who came were of the better sort; as we find many of them believed. Their presence is mentioned to do away with all doubt of the real death of Lazarus.[2]

In many ancient cultures, it is tradition to come together when death strikes. Communities gather around the bereaved family, offering food and support and love. The Orthodox Christian tradition includes memorials, prayer services at which families offer kollyva and pray for the deceased together, as a parish community. On the third day, on the fortieth day, and on the anniversaries to come, the community surrounds the bereaved family again and again.

Traditions like these feel foreign in our American culture, where it is growing ever more common to push death aside. Rather than dying at home, our loved ones die in hospitals and are rushed off to morgues. When my own father died, a very modern

---

2   Chrysostom, Homily on John 11.

American scene unfolded: My family avoided the dark, somber idea of a "funeral" and arranged a *celebration of life,* scheduling it many weeks after his death, when it was easier because they would be feeling better, more ready to interact with people. The community and the extended family were not invited into their pain and sorrow, but were held at bay while they grieved alone. The community gathered to celebrate joyfully later, when the morbid and difficult part was finished. Grief was for solitude, and company for celebration. The contrast with our Orthodox traditions was striking and profound.

The old traditions recognize the importance, the gravity and finality of death, and provide opportunities for communities to gather and support the bereaved. Mary and Martha experienced this, for as St. John said, their particular companions were of "the better sort"—the kind of people who show compassion and love even in disagreement.

Imagine one of those women who came from Jerusalem. Maybe she disapproved of Jesus and was worried that her friends were mixed up with him. But when she heard that Lazarus had died, she headed directly to Bethany. Maybe her myrrhbearing instinct to help with his burial, to offer food and comfort to his family, overrode any concerns about this false prophet he had befriended. While some of the people from Jerusalem were skeptical of Jesus and would later report His great miracle to the Pharisees, John tells us that "many of the Jews who had come to Mary, and had seen the things Jesus did, believed in Him" (John 11:45). Perhaps the ones who were real myrrhbearers, who had come out of pure love to serve Lazarus and his sisters, had hearts that were prepared to receive Christ. Perhaps all that loving service softened them, enabling them to recognize God when He walked up to them that day in Bethany. Recall that John Chrysostom said that "almsgiving is the mother of love, of that love, which is the characteristic of Christianity, which is greater than all miracles, by which the disciples of Christ are manifested."[3]

Perhaps it was through this caregiving that their hearts could truly see and hear Him—and thus new disciples of Christ were manifested in Bethany on that day. Through this simple service of caring for the dead, feeding the bereaved family, and mourning with those who mourn, we enter into communion with one another and with our Lord.

---

3   Chrysostom, "Homily 6" on Titus, https://www.newadvent.org/fathers/240162.htm.

FOR REFLECTION

- When a person is grieving, do you feel like you have no words to stop the pain? Does that stop you from offering your presence, or do you go to them anyway?

- Our daily lives are filled with work and distractions. Are you able to pull away from these things to take care of someone who is grieving or struggling in another way? Have you found yourself waving off someone in need because the details of day-to-day life consumed you?

- When has someone joined you in your grief, sitting beside you in the pain? How did that companionship change the experience?

I AM THE RESURRECTION

Lazarus died, and our Lord did not come.

People poured in from Jerusalem, the body was prepared—and still Jesus did not come.

They held a funeral, they went to the tomb to bury their brother, and still our Lord did not come.

From a distance, Jesus declared that Lazarus's death was for the glory of God. But no one told Mary and Martha that. They had no idea that death would not have the final word. They cared for their brother and buried him as if this were any other death, offering up their myrrhbearing service in various ways and receiving the love of their community. Little did they know that God was preparing their hearts to receive something bigger, and that the moment of revelation had arrived.

As Christ approached, Martha was the first to run out to meet Him, saying, "Lord, if You had been here, my brother would not have died. But even now I know that whatever You ask of God, God will give You" (John 11:21–22). It's such an interesting combination of rebuke and faith: Martha reminds Him that she called for Him, yet He didn't come. He didn't protect her heart from breaking. And yet, she still believes in Him; her love and her faith remain strong.

Isn't that where a faithful Christian lands after such a loss? *Lord, I asked You for a miracle, and You didn't deliver it, but I'm not going to budge. I am going to cling to You, even now.* Like Peter, all we can do is say, "Lord, to whom shall we go? You have the words of eternal life. Also we have come to believe and know that You are the Christ, the Son of the living God" (John 6: 68–69).

This is a true leap of faith, to hold tightly to God even when we don't understand Him.

Faith Beyond Comprehension

As Jesus and Martha talked, her understanding did not seem to grow. He told her, "Your brother will rise again," and Martha responded, "I know that he will rise again in the resurrection at the last day" (John 11:23-24).

Though Jesus meant that Lazarus would rise again *today*, Martha assumed that He was referring to the general resurrection, at the end of days. Her response revealed that she did not understand Him, but it also showed the strength of her faith: Unshaken by Christ's slow response, she *knew* that her brother would rise on the last day.

Martha, a perfect role model for each of us, ran to Christ and offered both her grief and her faith to Him. It is so tempting to blame God when loved ones die, or to doubt Him when He doesn't answer our call to save them. But when we are able to hold tight to our faith, to Christ, when we can run to offer Him our grief and even our frustration, He reveals Himself to us in new ways: "Jesus said to her, 'I am the resurrection and the life. He who believes in Me, though he may die, he shall live. And whoever lives and believes in Me shall never die. Do you believe this?'" (John 11:25–26).

As familiar as these words are to us today, this is actually the only time Jesus ever said, "I am the resurrection." It's a tremendous statement, made only to Martha—not to Peter or James or John, and not to Mary who sat at His feet, but to Martha, who had once been worried and troubled about many things. Jesus responded to her sincere offering with an entirely new insight into His true identity: He *is* the resurrection. It is not merely that Jesus can call down life from the Father, and it's not just that He is filled with life, but that He actually *is* life.

Martha reacts to this somewhat incomprehensible revelation by recognizing that God is in it; Martha knows that God is incomprehensible to her humble human mind, so she neither argues nor asks for explanation, but instead she said, "Yes, Lord, I believe that You are the Christ, the Son of God, who is to come into the world" (John 11:27).

Martha's response fascinates me, in part because she does not exactly address what it might mean for Jesus to *be* the resurrection. How can any of us process that exactly? How can the Man before her actually *be* life, and what does that mean to a woman who just buried her brother? Without questioning, Martha accepts what she cannot understand and recognizes that if Jesus is the resurrection, then He has to be the Son of God, the One, the Messiah.

She calls Him the One "who is to come into the world."[1] We might expect Martha to say that Christ *had finally come* into the world, after they had waited so long for Him. But in the original Greek, it is clear that she said He is the One "who *is coming*," recognizing something eternal and continuous in His movement to earth. In the Book of Revelation, St. John refers to Jesus as "the One who is and who was and who is to come" (Rev. 11:17). For

---

1   While many English translations will say "who is to come" or "who comes" or "who has come" into the world, in the original Greek, the present participle (is coming) is used: ὁ εἰς τὸν κόσμον ἐρχόμενος.

thousands of years, the Messiah was expected and anticipated. And since His Ascension into heaven, we have been waiting for His return. We know that He is always here, always with us—and yet it is also true that He is always coming, always on His way, always expected.

Long ago, the rabbis would end some prayers with, "Blessed be the name of his glorious kingdom forever." To most, *forever* meant into the eternal future, but to the Sadducees, who insisted that there was no afterlife, *forever* was said to mean "until this age ends." In order to combat this false belief and to emphasize the ongoing nature of God's Kingdom, the Pharisees changed the ending to "forever and ever" or "unto ages of ages," emphasizing that there would be more ages after this one.[2] Christians, also believing in the resurrection and in the eternal nature of God's Kingdom, used this formula to refer to this present age and also to the age to come: "now and ever and unto ages of ages." We glorify God now, and also into the eternal future, for always.

We believe in Jesus Christ, so we believe in the resurrection and the life. Jesus tells us that "the Kingdom of God is at hand" (Mark 1:15), so close that we can touch it. He says, "the Kingdom of God is within you" (Luke 17:21). His Kingdom is here on earth, and during our time in this world, He comes to us with His grace and His peace, offering a foretaste of heaven. After our bodily deaths we enter into heaven, but even this is not the final destination. Eventually, in the general resurrection at Christ's Second Coming, everything will be resurrected: "a new heaven and a new earth" will appear (Rev. 21:1). Forever and ever, unto ages of ages. There always seems to be more ahead. Whatever joy and peace we know

---

2   David Istone-Brewer, *Traditions of the Rabbis from the Era of the New Testament*, 2 vols. (Eerdmans, 2004).

in this world can be expected to increase, to just keep coming, more and more, through the ages of ages.

In our own lives, we call out to our Lord, and He comes to us, again and again. Mary and Martha waited for Christ to come, but He took His time. God acts when He acts, and we can't rush Him. But even when He is slow, Jesus always is coming. He is here among us, and yet, He is also always in motion toward us, knocking at the door of our hearts. Jesus revealed Himself to Martha: "I am the resurrection and the life." We are always waiting for the resurrection that is to come, for the life that is to come. What we enjoy on earth is a foretaste of heaven, and even what happens in heaven is a foretaste of the eventual Kingdom (the "and ever" of forever and ever). We can be frustrated by the waiting, angry that what we anticipate never seems to get here, or we can savor those little foretastes of holiness, treasuring the life He has already given us and anticipating the ways we can expect that life to continually grow in abundance.

FOR REFLECTION

- How do you process Christ's statement, "I am the resurrection and the life"?

- Many of St. John's writings emphasize Christ's continual coming toward us. In the Book of Revelation we read, "Behold, I stand at the door and knock. If anyone hears My voice and opens the door, I will come in to him and dine with him, and he with Me" (Rev. 3:20). He is on His way, coming to us, knocking at the door. Have you become familiar with the sound of His knock?

- If Christ is knocking, how do we let Him in? How do we receive Him?

JESUS WEPT

When the magi brought myrrh to present to the Christ Child, their gift pointed to the characteristic that most proves His humanity: He is born into death. This is the one experience that absolutely every human being will share, the one thing that unites us all. After the death of His friend Lazarus, as He approached the group of grieving women, Jesus entered our experience of death in another way: When He saw Mary and the crowd around her weeping, "He groaned in the spirit and was troubled" (John 11:33). What a beautiful phrase: "He groaned in the spirit." When He saw them grieving the loss of Lazarus, their grief ignited a grief in Him. "The Lord is near those who are brokenhearted" indeed, and He mourns with us (Ps. 33:19/34:18).

As he describes the crowd's approach toward Lazarus's tomb, John offers us the shortest, simplest verse in the Bible: "Jesus wept" (John 11:35). For so many people who grieve the loss of loved ones, this is a powerful statement. Too many Christians want to push down the pain of grief, to declare that because death is the portal to heaven, we should feel the joy of the departed's reunion with God rather than the pain of the loss. But even as we are relieved that the suffering is over and even as we hope that our loved ones rest in our Lord's embrace, the truth is that *death hurts*.

Weeping with Those Who Weep

We were not created for death; God created us for eternal life. When a loved one dies, we feel the unnaturalness of it. The bonds we share, the love between us, were not made to be broken. When death steals away our loved one, when those eternal bonds are ripped apart, the pain we feel is very real. Christ weeps with us, He joins us in the dark places, and He sits with us. He does not tell us to cheer up; He does not point to a bright side of our loss. He weeps with us, and this gives us a kind of permission to properly mourn every death, though we do not "sorrow as others who have no hope" (1 Thess. 4:13). Saint Cyril of Alexandria explains Christ's tears:

> Our Lord mourns more than just the death of Lazarus:
> And the Lord weeps, seeing the man made in His own image marred by corruption, that He may put an end to our tears. For this cause He also died, even that we may be delivered from death. . . . And the Jews thought that He wept on account of the death of Lazarus, but He wept out of compassion for all humanity, not bewailing Lazarus only, but understanding that which happens to all, that the whole of humanity is made subject to death, having justly fallen under so great a penalty.[1]

Our Lord weeps for every death; He weeps because He created mankind for life, and yet we have invited sin and death into this world. He weeps because we die, and He dies to destroy death's power over us.

As we become more like Him, we weep for mankind, too. We mourn the corruption and the death we see around us; we mourn

---

1   St. Cyril of Alexandria, Commentary on John 11.

for our own sinfulness and for the sins and pains of others. This is part of the Christian life, for—as Paul writes—we are called to "rejoice with those who rejoice, and weep with those who weep" (Rom. 12:15). We are called to a special kind of myrrhbearing service: the ministry of presence. As our Lord joins us in our sorrow, we join the sorrow of the world. We enter into a kind of communion, sharing each other's burdens and celebrating each other's joys. While it is true that death separates us from those we love, when we are able to offer up our grief to Christ and to one another, death can also bring us together. We gather in our grief, and we cling closer to our Lord in our pain.

FOR REFLECTION

- What does it mean to you to know that Jesus weeps with us?

- So often, when we grieve a misfortune or loss, we want someone to blame and we turn our anger on God. Are you able to turn to Him and invite Him into your grief, allowing Him to weep with you?

- Our Lord weeps with all of us in our grief. Are you able to join Him, to weep with Christ over the pain of those He loves? Is it natural to you to weep for strangers, or even for your enemies?

LAZARUS, COME FORTH!

When finally the moment arrived for Jesus to perform the truly unexpected and amazing miracle of raising Lazarus, to demonstrate His absolute power over death and corruption, the crowd of mourners led Him to the tomb. He asked them to roll away the stone, and then He cried out, "Lazarus, come forth!" (John 11:43). Jesus didn't touch the body or lay hands upon Lazarus to awaken him. Instead, He simply spoke to him. The Word offers words, calling Lazarus by name. Lazarus, who was by now surely in Hades, heard Jesus calling him, and he obeyed. Was Hades within earshot of Bethany? Or is this what the Psalmist means when he writes,

> Where could I go from Your Spirit,
> Or flee from Your face?
> If I should ascend into heaven, You would be there;
> If I should descend into Hades, You would be there.
>
> (Ps. 138/139:7–8)

There is nowhere we can go to escape the reach of our Lord. And there is nowhere He would not go to retrieve us. Even in Hades, Christ's voice rings out, loud enough to get Lazarus's attention immediately. Cyril of Alexandria expresses this scene so beautifully:

O the marvel! The ill-smelling corpse, even after the fourth day from death, He brought forth out of the tomb; and him that was fettered fast and bound hand and foot, He commanded to walk! And immediately, the dead man started up, and the corpse began to run, being delivered from its corruption and losing its bad smell, and escaping through the gates of death, and without any hindrance to running being caused by the bonds. And although deprived of sight by the covering which was over his face, the dead man runs without any hindrance towards Him Who had called him, and recognises the masterful voice. For Christ's language was God-befitting and His command was kingly, having power to loose from death, and to bring back from corruption, and to exhibit energy beyond expression.[1]

Called to Action

Lazarus heard Christ's command, and not only did he comply by walking, but as St. Cyril sees it, he was so eager to come to His Lord that "the corpse began to run." He would be freed from his fetters, and from corruption and the terrible stink of death, "escaping through the gates" that Christ would soon break forever. I love this vision of Lazarus, running for freedom, running for his life, running toward the voice of His beloved Lord. As St. Cyril describes it, Lazarus is decidedly *active*. There is no doubt that Jesus performed this miracle—and yet it is also true that He was not the only one exerting effort. Lazarus was no passive recipient; Christ commanded him to come forth, and Lazarus walked right out of that tomb.

Christ often required work from those who received miraculous healings. At the wedding at Cana, "His mother said to the

---

1   St. Cyril of Alexandria, Commentary on John 11.

servants, 'Whatever He says to you, do it'" (John 2:5), and they followed Christ's instructions. When He encountered the widow of Nain's son, "He came and touched the open coffin, and those who carried *him* stood still. And He said, 'Young man, I say to you, arise.' So he who was dead sat up and began to speak. And He presented him to his mother" (Luke 7:14–15). While of course Christ is accomplishing the miracle on His own, He asks the recipient to do some of the work. Lazarus is not transported from Hades, but walks—or perhaps as St. Cyril said, runs—back to his family. Likewise, we might well expect that if God works a miracle in our own lives, He may require us to take a leap of faith—to take action before we know that we'll have the strength and ability to complete the task at hand. Indeed, He demands things we really cannot do on our own. The paralytic could not stand up, and Lazarus could not come forth—but Christ called them to it, and suddenly, they could. Together with Christ, the impossible became possible. When it is Christ who calls us to it, nothing will be able to stop us. No gates will hold us when, like Lazarus, we respond with faith and hope, running to Him.

FOR REFLECTION

- In the services for Lazarus Saturday, we sing, "Calling Lazarus by name, Thou has broken in pieces the bars of hell and shaken the power of the Enemy."[2] When Christ raised Lazarus from the dead, the apparent strength of Hades began to show signs of strain. What must it have been like in Hades for all the righteous dead gathered in Abraham's bosom, when they heard Jesus' command and saw Lazarus run back to life?

- Have you ever experienced or witnessed miracles that required a work of obedience?

- Have you encountered anyone who assumes that if human work was involved, an answered prayer wasn't a miracle? How would you respond?

---

2   From the service of the Great Compline for Lazarus Saturday, from *The Lenten Triodion*, translated from the original Greek by Mother Mary and Archimandrite Kallistos Ware (St. Tikhon's Monastery Press, 2002), 467.

TO BIND AND TO LOOSE

Lazarus burst forth from the grave, "bound hand and foot with graveclothes"—like a slave to sin and death (John 11:44). His flesh was restored, the corruption his body had undergone was reversed, and life flowed through his veins once more. But Lazarus was still bound. He was not yet free.

Christ commanded Lazarus to come forth, and Lazarus made the choice to obey, to run toward the voice of our Lord. Then Christ gave one more command: "Loose him, and let him go" (John 11:44). One more task was needed in order to complete the work of Lazarus's resurrection, and Jesus commanded the community to do it. The work of Jesus is to bring life, and the work of the congregation is to unbind one another from the graveclothes that bind. The very people who served as Lazarus's myrrhbearers were asked just a few days later to undo their work; those who had wrapped him were now amazed to find themselves unbinding him.

Finding His Image

What does it look like to reach out to unbind another person? When God places someone in our path who is bound up by sin, how will we do our part to liberate him? In Bethany, the crowd had to choose to believe that under those wrappings was a living man, and then they had to distinguish, to separate, the clothes of death from the living man beneath them. Are we able to do that? Can we look at the sinner beside us and see a child of God, created in His image, underneath the wrappings of sin? And when we learn to distinguish the image of God even in people who are being overtaken by sin and death, how can we help them to see themselves— to find that they are more than just their graveclothes?

In the Gospel of Matthew, Jesus tells His apostles twice that "whatever you bind on earth will be bound in heaven, and whatever you loose on earth will be loosed in heaven." (Matt. 16:19; 18:18). He grants His apostles (and the Church He establishes through them) the authority to forgive sins, promising absolution in the Kingdom. The Church practices this spiritual unbinding in the Sacrament of Confession, where sins loosed on earth also are loosed in heaven.

Christ also called the community to unbind Lazarus, and we, as the larger Church community, are called to the same task. When we encounter a human being bound in the wrappings of sin and death, He calls us to unbind them. Like the community who had to peer through Lazarus's graveclothes to see a living man inside, can we discern a child of God, or do we see only their iniquities, identifying them with their sins? Is he *a thief,* or is he a human being who stole something? Is she *a liar,* or is she one of God's children who, in this instance, chose not to tell the truth? The way we see other people influences how they understand themselves— and when we gossip, when we spread stories about the crimes of others, we bind people to their sins. Perhaps unbinding is even part of the process of forgiveness: If someone harms us, could the way we think about them and about their actions be binding them?

On the other hand, when we look into someone's eyes and see the icon of Christ within, then we begin to loosen the knots. When we receive people as fellow broken humans on this difficult road, we start to pull at sin's hold on them. We cannot bring someone back to life or make them change their ways, but that's not what Christ asks. We simply are asked to see what He sees—the beautiful, living soul within. Perhaps when we see others as children of God, loving them as He does, they too will get a glimpse of how much God loves them. Only Christ's love will resurrect them, but if we can purify our own hearts, we may begin to radiate that love and become instruments in the transformation God is so ready to bring about.

FOR REFLECTION

- Who do you know whose freedom is restricted by the grave-clothes of sin and death that bind them?

- Does the community around them help free them, or bind them ever more tightly?

- Is there anyone in your life whom you might be binding? Anyone you are loosing?

ANOINTING FOR THE
DAY OF BURIAL

M ary and Martha appear in the Scriptures three times: first, when they host Jesus in their home, then when He comes to resurrect their brother, and finally, when Jesus returns to dinner at their house. This final time, the sisters are not quarreling. John tells us that they made Him a meal, and Martha served Him (John 12:2). How interesting that the sisters worked together on the meal, but Martha alone serves—and yet, she does not complain. We see no sign of a voice in her head, ranting about her sister's negligence. And Mary, for her part, does something different: No longer merely sitting at Christ's feet, she takes bold action: "Then Mary took a pound of very costly oil of spikenard, anointed the feet of Jesus, and wiped His feet with her hair. And the house was filled with the fragrance of the oil" (John 12:3).

Mary literally bore myrrh for Christ: She bought expensive, perfumed oil to anoint His body. Martha honored His body by serving Him a carefully prepared meal, nourishing Him in her home. The two sisters made love manifest in real, practical actions. Saint Cyril of Alexandria praises them: "While Martha was serving, Mary anointed the Lord with ointment, thus accomplishing her love towards Him; and by the actions of both, the measure of love was filled up and made perfect."[1]

Myrrhbearing as Offering and Prophecy

The sisters' actions are no longer opposed to one another. They do not debate whether they should anoint Christ's feet or serve Him at the table: The two actions are in harmony with one another. The combination of these two myrrhbearing actions, anointing and feeding, tangible worship and practical care, fill up "the measure of love."

Mary's action in particular is remarkable and also instructive: She washes our Lord's feet, a humble act of service for an honored guest. We must also be ready to humbly serve our Lord when He comes to us in the form of those in need—as the least of these. Indeed, on the evening before His Crucifixion, our Lord will soon wash the feet of His disciples, saying, "If I do not wash you, you have no part with Me" (John 13:8). We must be humble and vulnerable enough both to serve and to accept service, to love and to accept love. After washing their feet,

> He said to them, "Do you know what I have done to you? You call Me Teacher and Lord, and you say well, for so I am. If I then, *your* Lord and Teacher, have washed your feet, you also ought to wash one another's feet. For I have given you an example, that you should do as I have done to you. Most assuredly, I say to you, a servant is not greater than his master; nor is he who

---

1   St. Cyril of Alexandria, *Homilies on Luke*, Sermon 69, https://www.tertullian.org/fathers/cyril_on_luke_07_sermons_66_80.htm#SERMON%20LXIX.

is sent greater than he who sent him. If you know these things, blessed are you if you do them. (John 13:12–17)

Jesus is very clear: We must wash one another's feet. We must humble ourselves and serve one another in the simplest, most practical ways. It is good to "know these things," but we are not blessed by knowledge alone; instead, we are "blessed" if we do these things—if we put service into action, if we manifest love in real and practical ways.

Mary did not just wash our Lord's feet. She sacrificed incredibly expensive oil, worth more than a year's wages, to perform this act of worship. She was lavish and unthinkably generous in her offering. Such an alabaster flask often served as a woman's dowry, and indeed in the Song of Songs, the bride brings her spikenard to her beloved groom (1:12). If this was Mary's dowry (and we really don't know whether it was) then the offering was especially dear, as she would have been giving up the possibility of marriage and children, making something like a monastic vow to our Lord. Mary held back nothing in her offering: She used the finest oil available and wiped his feet with her own hair. Like the widow who gave two mites, she offered everything she had to our Lord.

But perhaps most amazingly, Jesus conferred even more meaning into her action: "She has kept this for the day of my burial. For the poor you have with you always, but Me you do not have always"[2] (John 12:7–8). Mary's loving act of service and worship suddenly was something more: She was not merely a woman

---

2   Saint Nikolai Velimirovich noted that Christ foresaw that He would receive no other anointing; this is His one and only proper burial anointing; for when Joseph and Nicodemus hurried to bury Him, they had no time before sundown to anoint Him, and when the women arrived in the early morning hours to do it, it was already too late, as He had risen.

serving her Lord, but Jesus' words revealed that her actions were a kind of incarnate prophecy, a preparation for His death.

The actions of these two sisters, now spiritually mature after living through the crucible of Lazarus's death and witnessing his resurrection, fill up the measure of love. They have grown into true myrrhbearers. They have become human beings who simply operate out of love at all times—people who can now be filled up with the love of Christ and radiate that love to those around them.

FOR REFLECTION

- What differences do you see in Martha and Mary, after going through these profound experiences around the death of Lazarus?

- Mary held nothing back—she spared no expense, offering up the oil and also her own hair in humble service. What would that look like in your life? What would be a lavish offering to our Lord from you?

- Mary made this offering, and Christ proclaimed her a prophet. In the Liturgy, we offer up bread and wine, and He gives us His Body and Blood. Christ regularly transforms our smaller offerings into something greater. When have you seen this in your own life?

WHAT MESSIAH IS THIS?

Jesus brought His disciples into the garden and asked them to keep watch while He prayed.[1] Once, twice, three times Jesus came back to them to find them asleep. He began to scold them the third time, but before the words came out of His mouth, officers entered to make the arrest. Judas gave Him away with a kiss, and they moved in. Peter, who had boldly walked out to meet Jesus on the water, saw the arrest taking shape. He recognized the moment: The time had come for Jesus to take His rightful place as the King of Israel, and the opening battle was beginning. Peter didn't hesitate—he took immediate action, his sword moving smoothly and instinctively to slice the ear off the high priest's servant. Ready to serve as a general in Christ's army, Peter was fighting valiantly for the new King of Israel.

Silent as a Lamb

What confusion must have filled Peter's heart when Jesus said, "Put your sword into the sheath. Shall I not drink the cup which My Father has given Me?" (John 18:11). *What cup? What fate? How could His fate be anything but taking His seat on the throne?* Peter had to watch Jesus heal this man's ear and allow Himself to be taken

---

1   See Matthew 26:36–75.

into custody, like a lamb to slaughter. Just a few short years ago in his boat, with nets full of fish, following Jesus seemed like a bold move. But suddenly everything had changed: Following Jesus now meant standing helpless beside our suffering Lord. It meant being identified not with power and victory, but with humiliation, exhaustion, suffering, and defeat. Peter just couldn't do it. As Fr. Alexander Schmemann writes,

> What we do know is that Christ's disciples, all of them, ran away and left him behind. Peter denied him three times. Judas betrayed him. Crowds followed Christ while he was preaching, and each person was expecting to get something from him: they expected help, miracles and healings; they expected liberation from hated Roman occupation; they expected him to put their earthly cares in order.[2]

Peter, along with so many of Christ's followers, waited for the Messiah who would restore the Kingdom of Israel, who would take on the high priests and the centurions, overthrowing the Romans and reestablishing God's people.

And now there He was, hanging on a cross, quietly. Passively.

The crowds cried out, "If He is the King of Israel, let Him now come down from the cross" (Matt. 27:42) and "Aha! *You* who destroy the temple and build it in three days, save Yourself, and come down from the cross" (Mark 15:29–30)! Is that what Peter hoped for? *Take Yourself down off that cross, Lord!* Maybe Peter wanted a Messiah who would break free from His constraints, leaping off the Cross and crushing those who would have killed Him. But Jesus remained as silent as a lamb; He did not put up a

---

2   Alexander Schmemann, *The Celebration of Faith: Sermons* (St. Vladimir's Seminary Press, 1991), 133.

fight. If Peter expected a Messiah who would overthrow the government and establish an earthly reign, then he was being honest when he said, "Woman, I do not know him" (Luke 22:57), and quietly slinked away.

Truth be told, there had been warning signs. In those last weeks, Jesus began to hint at His coming demise. As Fr. Schmemann writes, "The crowds now began to hear him foretelling that, through this love, he would offer himself as a sacrifice. And the crowd began to thin, to melt away."[3] Peter was not alone in his disappointment and confusion. All those people who gathered around, who saw Jesus heal the multitudes and raise Lazarus from the dead, had come to see the conquering King who would overthrow the Romans and restore the Kingdom of Israel. They did not know what to make of this messiah, who could not save Himself, let alone all of Israel.

Love Stays

If we ask, "Who are the myrrhbearers?" the answer is clear: They are the ones who did not scatter. "There were also women looking on from afar, . . . who also had followed Him and ministered to Him when He was in Galilee" (Mark 15:40–41). The women stayed with our crucified Lord.

Our Lord is stripped down, naked, beaten, and humiliated. At the foot of the Cross, the women's deepest fears are stripped of their protective layers: *Is He not the Son of God? Will He not save Israel? Will they crucify me, too?* They must have been afraid that they had somehow failed, that Christ had failed. Despite that fear, and despite their deep sorrow and all the uncertainty of the moment, the women did not move. They did not scatter; they held

---

3   Schmemann, 133.

tight to Christ and to one another. Saint John later writes, "There is no fear in love; but perfect love casts out fear" (1 John 4:18). That's how they stayed through the fear: They loved Him so much.

Did these myrrhbearers understand something the others could not see? Did they know that Jesus was a different kind of king, fighting a different kind of battle? Surely not. Christ had spoken about rising from the dead, but no one understood what He was saying. Resurrection was so far outside the realm of their experience—they could not know that He was about to trample down death by death. They thought He was here to solve the problem of Israel's decline and didn't understand that He was here to solve the much bigger dilemma of death's stranglehold on mankind. They didn't understand why Christ went like a lamb, or how He could be the Messiah and also be the one who died on the Cross. In order to stay with Him to the end, they had to let that dream die—that vision of a messiah who would stand up and take the throne.

The myrrhbearers didn't develop this fearlessness all of a sudden. They had been practicing. They had walked away from the comforts of home, and they continually sacrificed their own comfort so that they could better serve Jesus and the disciples. They had been learning to die to themselves through small, daily acts of faithfulness, and so their hearts were able to let go of their assumptions and ideas of who Christ was and who they were. None of it mattered as much as their love for Jesus and their choice to act on that love continually. They knew that their beloved Lord suffered, and their love drew them to Him. They expected no reward for their endurance—for all they knew, He simply was dying a painful, humiliating, and shameful death. But their love held them fast. Father Schmemann writes, "They stood at the cross only because they loved Jesus, and in loving him, suffered with him. They did not leave his poor, tortured body, but did all that love has always done at the final separation."[4]

Love has always stood vigil at the side of the dying loved one; it always has entered into the suffering of others. This Messiah was not what Israel expected, but love knows only hope, and it does not waiver. The myrrhbearers' love grew out of the mystery of faith:

> Faith is not a matter of mere understanding, so it is not cultivated and does not grow simply through investigation or through study. Faith, as trust in God and abandonment of oneself to Him, is closely related to love, which is God Himself. When you love, when you offer as much as you can to others, to your brother—to Christ—and end up by offering your very self to God, then you know Him: you believe.[5]

The myrrhbearers did not understand what our Lord's Crucifixion meant, but they didn't have to make sense of it. Out of love, they simply continued to offer everything they could. And as is so often the case in times of terrible suffering and pain, the best thing they could offer was their presence at the foot of the Cross.

---

4   Schmemann, 135.
5   Archimandrite Vasileios, *Hymn of Entry* (St. Vladimir's Seminary Press, 2011), 25.

FOR REFLECTION

- When have you felt unable to understand what God was doing in a particular situation?

- Have you ever been tempted to stop following God because you could not understand why He was allowing something terrible to happen?

- Were you called to greater faith in that moment, or was it greater trust? Might it have been greater love?

O HAPPY TOMB

After hours of suffering on the Cross, as the women stood vigil and watched, "Jesus cried out again with a loud voice, and yielded up His spirit." (Matt. 27:50). And then, as Gregory the Theologian expresses so beautifully,

> Many indeed are the miracles of that time: God crucified; the sun darkened and again rekindled; for it was fitting that the creatures should suffer with their Creator; the veil rent; the Blood and Water shed from His Side; the one as from a man, the other as above man; the rocks rent for the Rock's sake; the dead raised for a pledge of the final Resurrection of all men; the Signs at the Sepulchre and after the Sepulchre, which none can worthily celebrate.[1]

This moment is so profound that it cannot be properly recounted: Creation itself reeled when it saw its Creator die on a cross, the sun hid and the dead rose. All order was overturned when the creatures executed their Creator.

---

1   St. Gregory Nazianzen, "On the Holy Pascha," Oration 45.1, trans. Charles Gordon Browne and James Edward Swallow, in *Nicene and Post-Nicene Fathers, Series Two*, vol. 7, rev. ed., ed. Kevin Knight (New Advent), https://www.newadvent.org/fathers/310245.htm.

Let Us Also Take the Body

In a smaller way, Joseph of Arimathea overturned everything in his own life, offering all of it up to Jesus Christ. Joseph was a rich man, a man of influence and a member of the Sanhedrin. This is a critical point, for as St. Jerome pointed out, "To a poor and unknown man, it would not have been possible to penetrate to Pilate, the representative of Roman power."[2] Joseph had considerable influence, and he traded it for one last favor:

> Now when evening had come, there came a rich man from Arimathea, named Joseph, who himself had also become a disciple of Jesus. This man went to Pilate and asked for the body of Jesus. Then Pilate commanded the body to be given to him. When Joseph had taken the body, he wrapped it in a clean linen cloth, and laid it in his new tomb which he had hewn out of the rock; and he rolled a large stone against the door of the tomb, and departed. (Matt. 27:57–60)

A true myrrhbearer, Joseph received the body of Christ and carefully wrapped Him. He offered his very own tomb to ensure an appropriately honorable burial.

We can imagine the love, and the fear, with which Joseph tenderly received the body of Christ. Blessed Theophylact suggests that we follow his lead:

> Let us also take the Body of Jesus, through Holy Communion, and place It in a tomb hewn out of a rock, that is, place It within a soul which always remembers God and does not forget Him.
>
> And let that soul be hewn from a rock, that is, from Christ Who is the Rock on which we are established. Let us wrap the

---

2   From the "Commentary on Matthew," St. Jerome (The Catholic University of America Press, 2008).

Body of Jesus in the linen, that is, let us receive It within a pure body. For the body is the linen and the garment of the soul. We must receive the divine Body of the Lord not only with a pure soul, but with a pure body as well. And we must wrap It and enfold It within ourselves, and not leave It exposed. For this Mystery is something veiled and hidden, not something to be exposed.[3]

What an interesting twist on the call for us to become myrrh-bearers. We receive the Body of Christ in the Eucharist, we wrap It in the fine linen of our soul's baptismal garment, washed clean in confession, and we place it carefully into the tomb that is our soul. We reenact Joseph's myrrhbearing work every time we receive Holy Communion.

Theophylact suggests that our souls are tombs, "hewn from a rock, that is, from Christ Who is the Rock," the chief cornerstone. There is a stability, a solidity in rock—but there is also a sense in which we are petrified, dead stone, until Christ transforms us.

We know that if we, like Joseph, offer up our tombs, our hearts, to Christ, He will do as He promised: "I will give you a new heart and put a new spirit within you; I will take the heart of stone out of your flesh and give you a heart of flesh" (Ezek. 36:26). Joseph offered up his tomb, and Christ made it the treasury of life. He offered up his position in Jerusalem, and Christ made him an apostle and a saint. For, as He promised, "whoever desires to save his life will lose it, but whoever loses his life for My sake will find it" (Matt. 16:25).

As the Orthodox hymns of Holy Saturday declare, "O happy tomb! It received within itself the Creator, as one asleep, and it was made a divine treasury of Life."[4] This is just as true of our own souls: We receive our Creator and are brought from death to life.

---

3   Bl. Theophylact on Matthew 27.
4   Holy Saturday Matins, *The Lenten Triodion*, trans. Mother Mary and Archimandrite Kallistos Ware (St. Tikhon's Monastery Press, 2002), 650.

FOR REFLECTION

- During Holy Week, time can feel upside down: In some parishes Vespers is celebrated in the morning and Matins in the evening. In what other ways does the Resurrection overturn the world?

- Have you ever found that by doing something hard, by picking up your cross, you became blessed with something so good that it overshadowed or even transformed the difficulty you faced?

- Has God sent unexpected rewards to you or to someone you love? When?

JUST BEFORE DAWN

The women awaited the end of Sabbath, and as soon as it was permissible—maybe just a moment before then—just as the sun was ready to rise on the horizon, they hurried to the Tomb. On Friday, they had stayed by His side throughout His crucifixion and death, watching Joseph receive the body and place Him in the Tomb. They weren't able to pull themselves away from our Lord in His suffering. They loved Him too much to let Him out of their sight. But when the sun began to set and the Sabbath was upon them, they had to obey God—the same love that bound them to Christ also bound them to follow God's law, to abide by the Sabbath restrictions. In love, they obeyed, but they did not forget. They obtained the spices they would need (Mark 16:1), and as soon as the new day began to break, they were on their way.

The tradition of using myrrh to prepare a body for burial is ancient, because myrrh covers the scent of death, slowing decay, staving it off for as long as possible. Bishop Maxim Veselinovich writes,

A Myrrh Bearing Woman brings her spices to the tomb to honor the body of Jesus, trembling and astonished. And with myrrh, she wants to show that she does not compromise with the body's decay and that the final purpose of the body is not its decay but life. This treatment of the Lord's body with myrrh shows us that love and tenderness is the only way to face death.

Death hurts love, and love reacts in this way, so it seems that in the end, with the resurrection, love will win and not separation, which death seeks.[1]

How beautiful! Myrrh is love's declaration that death will not win, that life will not end. The myrrhbearing women approach the Tomb with a stubborn hopefulness, a belief in life that cannot be stamped out even by the death of the Son of God Himself.

Encountering the Unexpected

And yet, when the women arrived at the Tomb, they would not find a body at all. Instead, they came upon a shocking scene:

Now after the Sabbath, as the first *day* of the week began to dawn, Mary Magdalene and the other Mary came to see the tomb. And behold, there was a great earthquake; for an angel of the Lord descended from heaven, and came and rolled back the stone from the door, and sat on it. His countenance was like lightning, and his clothing as white as snow. And the guards shook for fear of him, and became like dead *men*. (Matt. 28: 1–4)[2]

---

1   Bishop Maxim. From the description of his fine art work, *Myrrhbearers* (https://sebastianpress.org/myrrhbearer/).

2   Each of the four Gospels tells the story a bit differently. The authors list differing women by name, and in some cases there is no angel, or one, or two angels at the Tomb. It is possible that the authors emphasized the aspects of the story that seemed most important to them. Some scholars explain the discrepancy by suggesting that the authors related scenes that happened in succession: Chronologically, the earliest account would have to be Matthew's, for in his Gospel we see the angel arrive and move the stone away from the Tomb. We will assume that God allows this variety in the Scriptures for a reason—that perhaps we are not meant to know exactly how the events unfolded, but instead we humbly receive the intent and content of each author equally.

The earth rumbled violently, and the angel looked like "lightning." What a sight, and what a shock! The women arrived to a completely different scene than they expected. The guards "shook for fear" and "became like dead men"; surely the women also were terrified. They arrived in grief and love, prepared to serve our Lord's body as love has always done, only to be confused and shaken. Is that their reward for bearing myrrh to serve the Lord? Saint John Chrysostom's words from the Introduction are worth repeating here:

> For what purpose do the two Marys wait beside the sepulcher? As yet they did not fully know his greatness. They had brought ointments. They were waiting at the tomb, so that if the madness of the civil authorities should relax, they might go and care for the body. Do you see these women's courage? See their depth of affection? See their noble spirit in providing? See their noble spirit even to death? Let us men imitate these women! Let us not forsake Jesus in times of trial! These women exposed their lives so much for him even when he was dead, even as they had spent so much for him when he was alive. But we men, I repeat, neither feed him when hungry nor clothe him when naked. Seeing him begging, we pass him by. And yet if we might really behold him in the neighbor, we would divest ourselves of all our goods.[3]

The women's love and service did not flag when Jesus was on the Cross, and it did not end with His death. They were completely dedicated to His service at all times. Jesus said, "Assuredly, I say to you, inasmuch as you did it to one of the least of these My brethren, you did *it* to Me" (Matt. 25:40). We constantly are called to

---

3   St. John Chrysostom, *Homilies on the Gospel of St. Matthew*, 2 vols. (Veritatis Splendor Publications, 2012).

inexhaustible love for mankind—and not just an abstract love for mankind in general, but real, tangible love for the very person God has placed before us. Whether it is feeding the hungry, bringing myrrh and spices to prepare a body, or unbinding one another from the sin and corruption that hold us, when we serve Christ by serving another person, we reveal the icon of Christ within them.

A Countenance Like Lightning

God provides us with opportunities to worship Him all the time, by placing people with needs in our paths. Our efforts benefit those we serve, and they also transform our own hearts. But God's project is so much larger than that. On His last Thursday evening in the Garden, our Lord prayed for us:

> I do not pray for these alone, but also for those who will believe in Me through their word; that they all may be one, as You, Father, *are* in Me, and I in You; that they also may be one in Us, that the world may believe that You sent Me. And the glory which You gave Me I have given them, that they may be one just as We are one: I in them, and You in Me; that they may be made perfect in one, and that the world may know that You have sent Me, and have loved them as You have loved Me. (John 17:20–23)

The Holy Trinity is one in the most profound way: We cannot separate the Father from the Son or the Holy Spirit. Christ calls us to be "made perfect" and to become "one just as" the Holy Trinity is one. That may sound impossible, but He does say that He will give us the glory that He received from the Father; He will bestow gifts upon us that make even the most unimaginable transformation possible. We are called only to do our small part: Humbly serve the person in front of us—feed him, unbind him, visit him in his prison—and let God do the rest.

And so, very early in the morning, the myrrhbearing women show up at the Tomb. They do not fear the guards, and they do not fear being associated with the humiliated and crucified Christ. They are not concerned about how the Son of God possibly could have come to restore Israel then been executed before He accomplished it; they have no idea that the problem He came to solve was much larger than any nation. They do not understand, but they come anyway, despite the earthquake and the terrifying angel whose countenance is like lightning. They keep approaching the Tomb, single-mindedly working their way to their Lord so that they can continue to care for His body, as they had done for so long when He was alive. Their determination to serve Him outweighs everything else.

FOR REFLECTION

- The women built up a habit of selflessness and perseverance from years of serving Jesus and others. This momentum carried them through the Crucifixion and brought them to His Tomb at daybreak. How do the smaller habits of our daily lives set up momentum for us—for better or worse?

- So many things—fear, distraction, anxiety—could have kept the women from the Tomb, but did not. What keeps us from running to Christ, from witnessing unexpected evidence of His Resurrection?

- The women kept showing up, and they were rewarded. Has your persistence been rewarded? How?

RESURRECTION

The guards fell away "like dead men" (Matt. 28:4), but the women continued to approach the Tomb and the angel within it, until they heard him ask, "Why do you seek the living among the dead?" (Luke 24:5). Their minds must have reeled with the strangeness of those words. Why didn't the angel simply explain what happened? Instead, he asked this question, implying that somehow, the women *should know* this. He was accomplishing more than just *announcing* the Resurrection. He wanted the women to *recognize* the Resurrection that Jesus had taught them; He had prepared them for this moment. In the Gospel of Matthew, the angel says, "He is risen, *as He said*" (Matt. 28:6; emphasis mine). He states the message most clearly in Luke's Gospel:

> He is not here, but is risen! Remember how He spoke to you when He was still in Galilee, saying, 'The Son of Man must be delivered into the hands of sinful men, and be crucified, and the third day rise again.'" And they remembered His words. (Luke 24:6–8)

Prompted by the angel, they remembered. They were disciples of Christ; they learned at His feet, and He said He would rise again. They didn't understand what He meant at the time, but now, with the angel's help, they made the connection. The fact that Jesus told them in advance that He would rise again confirmed that He chose to enter into death. His Crucifixion was not His defeat. This was all part of the plan, a necessary step toward victory.

Only the women—not Joseph of Arimathea or Nicodemus, not John or any of the disciples—came to the Tomb early that morning. They had spent so many years taking care of Christ, they had developed a habit of serving Him that propelled them forward even as the sun was barely rising. They served Him in life, and they stood beside Him, sharing in the pain of His Crucifixion, and now they were about to walk into His Tomb to care for His body. Their ongoing, tangible love earned them a very special place in history. They were granted the joy of being the first witnesses to the Resurrection of Christ!

Crucified with Christ

All Christians eventually must follow the path of the myrrhbearing women. We must learn to serve one another, and we must enter into His Crucifixion so that we too will be granted something entirely new and beautiful:

> Or do you not know that as many of us as were baptized into Christ Jesus were baptized into His death? Therefore we were buried with Him through baptism into death, that just as Christ was raised from the dead by the glory of the Father, even so we also should walk in newness of life.
>
> For if we have been united together in the likeness of His death, certainly we also shall be *in the likeness* of *His* resurrection, knowing this, that our old man was crucified with *Him,* that the body of sin might be done away with, that we should no longer be slaves of sin. (Rom. 6:3–6)

If we can enter into the "likeness of His death," then we will also come into "the likeness of His resurrection." Indeed, Jesus said to

Martha, "I am the resurrection and the life." He is life and cannot be held by the power of death. What can that mean? What is it to be resurrected with Christ? In his first epistle, Saint John writes:

> We know that we have passed from death to life, because we love the brethren. He who does not love *his* brother abides in death. Whoever hates his brother is a murderer, and you know that no murderer has eternal life abiding in him.
>
> By this we know love, because He laid down His life for us. And we also ought to lay down *our* lives for the brethren. But whoever has this world's goods, and sees his brother in need, and shuts up his heart from him, how does the love of God abide in him?
>
> My little children, let us not love in word or in tongue, but in deed and in truth. (1 John 3:14–18)

To be resurrected, to be filled with this new life, is to open our hearts to our brothers and sisters in need, showing our love "in deed and in truth." We have come full circle: to be resurrected is to become a myrrhbearer.

Love Itself

As St. John wrote in his epistle, "God is love" (1 John 4:8). God's very being, His existence as a community of three persons, is constituted by love; He is actually love itself. As Christians, our goal is to be filled with His presence and to become ever more like Him—that is, to be filled with love, to become ever more like love, to become the very body of love itself. God is love, and as He told Martha, He is the Resurrection and the life. We cannot abide in one without the other, and so we find that love and resurrection and life are completely fused.

Humans love easily: We love our families; we love those who love us back; we especially love those who belong to us. But when we become more than individuals in the world, when we are grafted onto the Body of Christ, we are transformed. Through baptism, chrismation and the sacramental life of the Church, as we learn to empty ourselves out in service to others, something happens: We begin to love people who don't belong to us, even the ones who don't love us back. As Metropolitan John of Pergamon explained, the Christian loves everyone "out of the fact that his new birth from the womb of the Church has made him part of a network of relationships which transcends every exclusiveness."[1] This new birth, this new life, is to be filled with love and to begin together to become "one" as Christ prayed we would. To be filled with Christ means to love like Christ loves. This love allows us to grow in mystical communion with Him and with one another.

---

1   Met. John Zizioulas, *Receive One Another: 101 Sermons*, ed. Bishop Maxim Veselinovich, trans. Rev. Fr. Gregory Edwards (Sebastian Press, 2023), 58.

FOR REFLECTION

- Love and life are so bound up together that to hate my brother makes me a *murderer,* for in denying him love, I deny him life. Sin and death are one and the same, and love and life are the same. In what ways do you see evidence of this around you?

- Do you distinguish between loving people who love you back, and loving people who don't? Why is it so difficult to love those who don't return our love?

- Is it truly possible to love everyone as Christ did?

GO AND TELL YOUR BRETHREN

T he angel told the women that Jesus had risen "as He said," and they recognized that it was true: He did say that He would rise again, and only now were they beginning to understand what He meant. There was no time to ponder this in their hearts, as the angel immediately gave them an assignment:

"And go quickly and tell His disciples that He is risen from the dead." . . .

So they went out quickly from the tomb with fear and great joy, and ran to bring His disciples word.

And as they went to tell His disciples, behold, Jesus met them, saying, "Rejoice!" So they came and held Him by the feet and worshiped Him. Then Jesus said to them, "Do not be afraid. Go *and* tell My brethren to go to Galilee, and there they will see Me." (Matt. 28:7–10)

The women obeyed the angel and were rewarded with the resurrected Christ Himself! Each Gospel tells the story a bit differently, but in each one the myrrhbearing women are instructed to "go and tell My brethren!" This is not the sort of news one keeps to oneself.

This news must be shared. And so the women obey, becoming the very first evangelists—the first to preach the gospel.

Witnesses

What an honor this is! These faithful women had walked away from the comfort of their homes, dying to their old lives and their plans. They served Christ and His followers humbly, and they learned at His feet, following Him to His death. They allowed neither discomfort nor fear to hold them back. This self-denial and loving service transformed them, until finally, on this morning, their love for Christ brought them to the Tomb at sunrise, where a reward awaited: They were the first witnesses of the Resurrection, and then they became the first to preach it.

There are many moments in the Scriptures when Jesus encounters a woman and, rather than keeping away from her as the Jewish culture demanded, He engages her. Jesus spoke with the Samaritan woman at Jacob's well, teaching her about the Living Water and about worshiping in spirit and truth—two important teachings, delivered only to her. Photini, as she would come to be known, ran back to town to preach to her community, preparing them to receive Jesus. The townspeople were curious:

> So when the Samaritans had come to Him, they urged Him to stay with them; and He stayed there two days. And many more believed because of His own word.
>
> Then they said to the woman, "Now we believe, not because of what you said, for we ourselves have heard *Him* and we know that this is indeed the Christ, the Savior of the world." (John 4:40–42)

Photini got their attention and opened their eyes, but when they heard for themselves, they believed. All of us, whatever our place

in the world, may be called to preach—to bear witness to Christ—
the full responsibility never falls on us. Christ Himself reaches out
to every human being, revealing Himself and confirming the truth
of the gospel. Ultimately, we may point one another to Him, but
Jesus ministers to every one of us personally.

Similarly, when the myrrhbearing women preached the gospel
of the risen Christ to the disciples, they were preparing them to
understand the Resurrection. But the women's words alone weren't
enough to make the disciples believe:

> Then they returned from the tomb and told all these things to the
> eleven and to all the rest. It was Mary Magdalene, Joanna, Mary
> *the mother* of James, and the other *women* with them, who told
> these things to the apostles. And their words seemed to them like
> idle tales, and they did not believe them. (Luke 24:9–11)

The women preached the Resurrection, but the apostles did
not initially believe them. Peter and John then ran to the Tomb
to see for themselves. Like Photini, they then called the others to
come and see. Even the greatest saints and apostles give us only
their own testimony and urge us to come to Him ourselves. In
the end, we help prepare others' hearts, and we point one another
in the right direction, but God does the real work. The Holy
Spirit reveals the truth to their hearts, and Christ Himself will
come to them.

Saint Augustine sees the divine hand of Providence in God's
choice of women to deliver the gospel, to become apostles to the
apostles:

> These things seemed in their eyes like an idle tale. How very
> unhappy is the human condition! When Eve related what
> the serpent had said, she was listened to straightaway. A lying

woman was believed, and so we all died. But [the disciples] didn't believe women telling the truth so that we might live. If women are not to be trusted, why did Adam trust Eve? If women are to be trusted, why did the disciples not trust the holy women? So in this fact we have to reflect on the goodness of the Lord's arrangements, because this, of course, was the doing of the Lord Jesus Christ that it should be the female sex which would be the first to report that he had risen again. Humanity fell through the female sex; humankind was restored through the female sex. A virgin gave birth to Christ; a woman proclaimed that he had risen again. Through a woman death, through a woman life. But the disciples didn't believe what the women had said. They thought they were raving, when in fact they were reporting the truth.[1]

Augustine sees God intentionally restoring honor to women: Eve sinned, and humanity has blamed all women for her choice, so God makes women the gateway to redemption and the messengers of the good news.

Photini's neighbors heard enough in her testimony to invite Jesus to stay a while, and the disciples heard enough in the women's idle tales to run to the Tomb to investigate. The Holy Spirit is the Spirit of Truth; it is only through Him that we can come to know Christ. You and I can bear witness, and we hope to intrigue those who do not know Him, but we cannot force real knowledge of Christ. We can announce Him, but the listener will need to open their hearts when He knocks and invite Him inside.

---

1   St. Augustine of Hippo, "Commentary on Luke 24," *New Testament III: Luke*, eds. Arthur Just Jr. and Thomas C. Oden, Ancient Christian Commentary on Scripture, vol. 3 (InterVarsity Press, 2003).

FOR REFLECTION

- Sometimes we forget that all we can do is inspire our brethren, our children, or our spouses to be open to Christ. Only God can speak to their hearts and transform them. Is there someone in your life who has taught you that lesson?

- This truth may be why so many saints suggest that we speak less and pray more. St. Porphyrios, for example, recognizes the limits of the power of our words and counsels parents, "Prefer prayer and speak to [your children] through prayer. Speak to God and God will speak to their hearts."[2] Are you able to follow that advice?

- What do you think works well to help others come to Christ? What gets in the way?

---

2   St. Porphyrios, *Wounded by Love: The Life and the Wisdom of Elder Porphyrios* (Denise Harvey, 2005).

Part Three

MYRRHBEARERS
IN ACTION

INTRODUCTION

In the first part of this book, we came to know the scriptural myrrhbearers—those people who braved Roman authority, daring to approach Christ's body to honor and care for Him. In the second part, we traced their story through the Gospels, locating a narrative that is, perhaps, the basic framework of the Christian life: We begin as individuals, looking out for ourselves and getting into scuffles, and then a change comes, and we begin to die to ourselves in order to serve others. In time, we find that we love Jesus and our neighbors with more and more of our hearts. The more we give up our lives, the more life we receive. The more we serve, the more we are transformed. As we die with Christ, dying to our own needs and preferences, and live for the other, we are born into new life. We become a different kind of person: one who is capable of deep communion and great love; one whose heart sings out in joy, even under difficult and painful circumstances.

In the final part of this book, we will look at the real-life examples of those who have come before us, who have run the race, and crossed the finish line (Heb. 12:1). The saints of the Church are examples of people who became one with the human race as the Holy Trinity is one, as our Lord so fervently prayed we would be. In particular, we will look at the lives of some wonderful caretaking saints who allow us to glimpse the perfected art of myrrhbearing and the transformative effect it has on our hearts. As always, God's saints are varied and complex, and they show many paths to grow into holiness. They each manifest myrrhbearing in different ways, and yet we will see similar threads running through their lives: asceticism and generosity, loving service to others, readiness to forgive, and a radical trust in God and His Providence. We will find diverse ways to live out this myrrhbearing mission, to make love incarnate. As we examine each unique example, seeing how myrrhbearing took shape in a particular life, it is my hope that we will begin to envision how myrrhbearing might look in our own lives.

TOBIT

The Book of Tobit is one of my very favorite parts of the Old Testament, but I hadn't even heard of it until I was in my thirties. It's not that I wasn't reading my Bible; it's just that Tobit wasn't in *my* Bible. It's not in a lot of Bibles,[1] and that's a shame because it really is a wonderful story and a moving example of myrrhbearing.[2]

Tobit, which means "the Lord is good" in Hebrew, was a very faithful Jewish man, a son of the tribe of Naphtali, from Thisbe in Galilee. Eight centuries before Christ, the Assyrian Empire took over the Northern Kingdom of Israel and much of the surrounding

---

1   As it happens, there are two different ways to build an Old Testament. Originally, there was the Septuagint, which is the version of the Old Testament that was in circulation during Jesus' time and that is used by the Orthodox and Roman Catholic Churches. Between the seventh and tenth centuries, a group of Jews known as the Masoretes copied, edited, and distributed an updated version of the Jewish Bible that left out a number of books, including Tobit. This leaves us with two different sets of books for the Old Testament: the Septuagint and the Masoretic. Because most Protestant Bibles are based on the Masoretic texts rather than the Septuagint, Tobit is missing from most English-language Bibles. Additionally, some find Tobit to be quite unbelievable—which opens up an interesting question about the various genres that are collected in the Bible and what they mean.

2   If you have never read Tobit, I encourage you to do so. It is a delightful, short, and easy read. And have no fear—there are no spoilers in this chapter! We will just scratch the surface of the beginning of the story.

regions, enforcing a mass deportation meant to assimilate these diverse groups to Assyrian society and ways of thinking. Tobit was among those taken to Media and Nineveh, where he lived in captivity among hostile people. He tells us that the rest of his tribe "ate from the bread of the Gentiles," (Tobit 1:10), assimilating into their pagan culture. Many of them worshipped Baal instead of God, but Tobit and his family remained faithful to the God of their Fathers.

Tobit must have felt very lonely, taken by force from his homeland and separated from his extended family and community. What's more, he lost his religious community as, one by one, his countrymen became part of the surrounding pagan culture. In our own times, many Christians can relate to this loneliness as they watch other believers walk away from God and embrace the ways of a modern and godless society. It is instructive, however, to consider how Tobit treats those who have fallen away:

> In the days of Shalmaneser, I did much almsgiving to my brothers. I would give my bread to the hungry and my clothing to the naked. If I saw anyone of my people dead, cast outside the wall of Nineveh, I would bury him. If King Sennacherib put someone to death when he came trying to escape from Judea, I buried them secretly. For in his anger, he put many to death, and the bodies were sought by the king; but they were not found. But one of the men of Nineveh went and made known to the king concerning my burying them. So I hid, and when I knew I was being sought to be put to death I was frightened and ran away. All of my possessions were seized and I had nothing left, except Anna my wife and Tobias my son. (1:16–20)

Tobit expressed his love for God by taking care of God's own people—even if they had turned away from Him. Tobit did not distinguish between those who remained faithful and those who did not. He didn't judge their actions but stubbornly loved the people whom God loved. He did not merely pray that they would come back to their senses and to their God, but he actively did "much almsgiving" by caring for the bodies of his brothers: feeding, clothing, and burying them. If our bodies are indeed temples of the Holy Spirit, then Tobit stopped and worshiped God, offering a sacrifice at every temple he encountered along his path.

Tobit was arrested for his good deeds, but through God's Providence he was allowed to return home. What should have been a festive welcome did not last:

> When I arrived at my house, my wife Anna and my son Tobias were given back to me. It was the Feast of Pentecost, which is the holy feast of the seven weeks. A good dinner was prepared for me, so I sat down at the table to eat. When I saw the abundance of meat, I said to my son, "Go and bring whomever you may find of our needy brethren who are mindful of the Lord. Behold, I will wait for you." (2:1–2)

Tobit had not sat at a table with his family in a very long time, and as a faithful man who had done nothing wrong, surely he deserved to enjoy a peaceful meal to celebrate a holy feast. But Tobit could not feast without inviting in the hungry. He was so accustomed to delaying and suppressing his own gratification in service to others that he didn't hesitate, but reflexively called for the hungry guests.

Tobias, Tobit's son, came home and said:

> "O father, one of our people was strangled and thrown into the marketplace."

So before I [Tobit] even tasted anything, I jumped up and carried the corpse into a room until sunset. Then I returned, bathed myself, and ate my bread in sorrow. (2:3–5)

Tobit hid the body until nightfall so that the man could be buried under cover of darkness. Touching the dead body made him ritually unclean, so the faithful Tobit further postponed his meal until he could complete a purification ritual. Finally he sat down to eat with his family, but the joy of reunion had already turned to sorrow—perhaps because of the death of this anonymous young man, but also because Tobit was once again obliged to endanger his freedom and even his life by breaking Assyrian law in order to serve God.

After dinner, Tobit went right back to work:

When the sun went down, I departed, and after digging a grave, I buried him. My neighbors laughed at me and said, "He is no longer afraid to be put to death for doing such a thing. He ran away before, and now, behold, he is burying the dead again." (2:7–8)

Tobit loved God and was unwavering in his obedience, and what was his reward? His neighbors mocked him, not recognizing any value in respectful burial. They did not care, as Tobit did, that the bodies of God's children, whether breathing or not, are precious to Him. What a lonely position for Tobit, isolated by the knowledge that his neighbors' understanding was so very far from his own.

Unfortunately, Tobit's misery was not soon relieved:

On the same night that I buried him, I returned home. But since I was defiled, I slept by the wall of the courtyard with my face uncovered. However, I did not see the sparrows on the wall, for while my eyes were open the sparrows discharged their droppings into my eyes, and they became white films in my eyes. I went to physicians, but they could not help me. (2:9–10)

Tobit buried the body to serve God and was too tired to bathe and purify himself again. He gave into sleep only to be blinded by sparrow dung. Poor, long-suffering Tobit! His miseries could have ended at any time, had he simply stopped following God. How much easier it would have been to eat dinner without inviting the poor inside, to shake his head at the sad news of a death without bothering to risk his life and livelihood, to simply rest in his own bed without first completing complex purification rituals. But Tobit would not forget God's commandments, and he would not turn his face away from the ones God loved.

Tobit's stubborn love is such a wonderful example for all of us. When everyone else abandoned God, Tobit stood firm. Though others saw no value in it, he insisted on feeding the poor and hungry and on honoring the dead, serving the bodies of God's beloved people. He constantly put his own comfort and safety aside to serve others—dying to himself to live out commandments of love. Every Jewish person thrown over the walls of Nineveh— even if he now worshiped other gods—was a child of God, and Tobit never forgot it. Even if the children of God forgot that they belonged to Him, Tobit did not. He saw them as brothers. So many of us, when faced with the apostasy of our friends, would be angry. Our pride would rear up and take over; we would bask in the importance of being the only good ones left, the remnant. Like children confident that they had become their father's favorite, we would look with disdain at those who had fallen away. But not Tobit. The very people he risked his life for were the ones who had forsaken God.

FOR REFLECTION

- When you see others fall away, whether from God or from some standard of virtue or excellence, do you find yourself judging them?

- Can you imagine putting your life on the line to honor those who are already dead or those who have apostatized, abandoning God to worship false gods?

- How stubborn is your love? Does the difficulty of doing the right thing cause you to give up too easily?

BASIL THE GREAT

Saint Basil came from an illustrious Cappadocian family of considerable wealth, remarkable intelligence, and deep Christian faith. His grandparents endured terrible persecutions, and his mother and most of his siblings were noted theologians and saints. Basil was a great intellectual of his day and the author of some of our most beautiful prayers—many of which are included in the Divine Liturgy bearing his name—as well as complex treatises and eloquent sermons.[1] But his most important work as a myrrhbearer was his creation of a dynamic Christian health center.

Basil studied in Constantinople and then in Athens, learning from the greatest philosophers of his time and mastering their precise language so that he could articulate the gospel with exactitude. Combined with asceticism and love of God, he would use what he learned to work out the great theological questions of his day. However, he found the pagan philosophies empty and even regretted studying them. He later wrote,

Much time had I spent in vanity, and had wasted nearly all my youth in the vain labor which I underwent in acquiring the

---

1 Biographical information comes from accounts in *The Prologue of Ohrid*, January 1, 2 Saint Basil the Great, Archbishop of Caesarea, and at https://www.oca.org/saints/live, January 1, Saint Basil the Great, Archbishop of Caesarea in Cappadocia.

wisdom made foolish by God. Then once upon a time, like a man roused from deep sleep, I turned my eyes to the marvelous light of the truth of the Gospel. . . . Then I read the Gospel, and I saw there that a great means of reaching perfection was the selling of one's goods, sharing them with the poor, giving up all care of this life, and the refusal to allow the soul to be turned by any sympathy to things of earth.[2]

Done with worldly knowledge and on his way to rejecting wealth, Basil went on pilgrimage, visiting the great desert monastics of the fourth century. From Palestine to Syria to Alexandria, he developed a deep admiration for the ascetics, saying, "I was amazed at their persistence in prayer and at their triumphing over sleep. They were subdued by no natural necessity, ever keeping their souls' purpose high and free, in hunger, in thirst, in cold, in nakedness."[3]

When we think of freedom, we do not always picture ourselves hungry and cold, living in a cave in the desert. We want comfort and security, full bellies and warm houses. But Basil found freedom in letting go of all those things—and the effort that it takes to sustain them—and leaving his soul truly free to contemplate God.

As the oldest son, Basil had inherited the majority of the family estate from his father. Basil then fulfilled the call he found in the Gospels: He gave away all his wealth to the poor. He liquidated his assets to feed those in need, and keeping just one garment for himself, he began to live in the wilderness near his old home.

---

2 St. Basil the Great, Ep. 223 "Against Eustathius of Sebastia," in *On Social Justice*, trans. C. Paul Schroeder, Popular Patristics Series 38 (St. Vladimir's Seminary Press, 2009), 18.

3 Isaac E. Lambertsen, Dimitriĭ, and Holy Apostles Convent, eds., *The Lives of the Three Hierarchs: Saints Basil the Great, Gregory the Theologian and John Chrysostom* (Holy Apostles Convent, 1998), 9.

Meanwhile, his sister, Macrina, and widowed mother, Emmelia, also had left their lives of luxury and started a monastery nearby, in the same wilderness. Famously, their former servants joined them, becoming nuns as well, and Macrina and Emmelia lived side by side as sisters with those who used to take orders from them. The family wealth was given to the poor, and Basil, Macrina, and Emmelia all gave themselves over to a far simpler life. They lived in poverty and prayer, and God richly rewarded their efforts. Basil wrote, "Quiet is the first step in our sanctification."[4] Away from the distractions of being illustrious leaders and managing their wealth—and from the constant work of preserving their comfort and warmth—they embraced the silence of the wilderness and found God in the stillness.

Called to Serve the Church

Back in the cities, the Church was embroiled in controversy as it struggled with the Arian heresy.[5] Basil was called back into action on this front, to serve as the bishop of Caesarea. He produced great theology and articulated brilliant defenses of the Faith. He was an excellent shepherd to his flock, for in addition to being a brilliant preacher and teacher, he took real care of his people.

During a terrible famine, Basil exhorted the wealthy to give what they had to feed the poor. His younger brother, Gregory of Nyssa, described how Basil personally directed and served:

Basil gathered together the victims of the famine . . . and set before men and women of every age, and even infants, basins of

---

4   *The Lives of the Three Hierarchs*, 11.
5   Arianism denied the divinity of Christ and taught that the Son of God was created by the Father.

soup and such meat as was found preserved among us, on which the poor live. Then imitating the ministration of Christ, Who, girded with a towel, did not disdain to wash the disciples' feet . . . he attended to the bodies and souls of those who needed it, combining personal respect with the supply of their necessity, and so giving them a double relief.[6]

Basil spoke with the people, offering love and spiritual leadership while providing food to sustain them. He cared for them personally, body and soul.

Basil grew this storehouse of food for the poor into something far larger, known as "the Basiliad" or the "New City." It is often considered one of the first hospitals, but it seems to have served many people in various ways: In addition to the hospital for the sick and the poor, Basiliad included a leprosarium to house and care for lepers and those with profound, lifelong infirmities, as well as rooms for travelers, physicians, cooks, and helpers. The bishop's residence was there, as were those of the clergy and monks who served beside him. Bishop Basil conceived the administrative organization and personally cared for the patients, even kissing the lepers when he greeted them. A chapel was built for divine services, and people came for religious instruction, learning the principles of simplicity and sharing. Indeed, "Basil himself counseled the monks who worked there to look after the patients as if they were brothers of Christ."[7] The Basiliad provided every kind of healing, satisfying physical needs, offering emotional support, and fulfilling the need for spiritual healing through the Sacraments and the liturgical life. The New City was much more than a place

---

6   *Lives of the Three Hierarchs*, 24.
7   Demetrios J. Constantelos, *Byzantine Philanthropy and Social Welfare*, Rutgers Byzantine Series (Rutgers University Press, 1968), 155.

for food and medical care—it was a holy place where those in need found not just assistance but also the love of Christ.

Gregory the Theologian, who also worked at the Basiliad, described this beautiful place in his funeral oration for Basil:

> Go forth a little way from the city, and behold the new city, the storehouse of piety, the common treasury of the wealthy, in which the superfluities of their wealth, aye, and even their necessaries, are stored, in consequence of his exhortations, freed from the power of the moth, (Matthew 6:19) no longer gladdening the eyes of the thief, and escaping both the emulation of envy, and the corruption of time: where disease is regarded in a religious light, and disaster is thought a blessing, and sympathy is put to the test.[8]

Basil convinced the wealthy to fund this great center of Christian service through the creation of a common treasury of "the superfluities of their wealth." Basil addressed excess wealth in many of his sermons. For example, he gave a famous sermon, "I Will Tear Down My Barns," about Christ's parable in Luke 12:16–21, saying,

> Who are the greedy? Those who are not satisfied with what suffices for their own needs. Who are the robbers? Those who take for themselves what rightfully belongs to everyone. And you, are you not greedy? Are you not a robber? The things you received in trust as a stewardship, have you not appropriated them for

---

8   St. Gregory Nazianzen, "Funeral Oration on the Great S. Basil, Bishop of Caesarea in Cappadocia," Oration 43, trans. Charles Gordon Browne and James Edward Swallow, in *Nicene and Post-Nicene Fathers, Series Two*, vol. 7, rev. ed., ed. Kevin Knight (New Advent), https://www.new advent.org/fathers/310243.htm.

yourself? Is not the person who strips another of clothing called a thief? And those who do not clothe the naked when they have the power to do so, should they not be called the same? The bread you are holding back is for the hungry; the clothes you keep put away are for the naked, the shoes that are rotting away with disuse are for those who have none, the silver you keep buried in the earth is for the needy. You are thus guilty of injustice toward as many as you might have aided, and did not.[9]

Basil's image of unused clothing and shoes rotting in the closet is convicting. How many of us own not just one or two pairs of shoes and a jacket in the closet, but uncounted items gathering dust? Did God give us so much because He desires that we share it? Basil argued that any excess possessions or funds were not intended for us; we are meant to take what we truly need and to distribute the rest.

Basil was not simply trying to make people feel guilty, or even trying to fill the coffers of his own charity. He spoke from experience: Basil grew up with excessive luxury and privilege. He knew what it was like to be rich, and he knew the freedom of throwing off the yoke of his wealth. He understood that possessions become an entanglement and begin to bind us. In his sermon, "To the Rich," he says,

If you had truly loved your neighbor, it would have occurred to you long ago to divest yourself of this wealth. But now your possessions are more a part of you than the members of your own body, and separation from them is as painful as the amputation of one of your limbs.[10]

---

9   From "I Will Tear Down My Barns," *On Social Justice*, 69–70.
10   From "To the Rich," *On Social Justice*, 43.

Attachment to wealth grows, and soon we cannot bear the idea of being without it. But as Jesus taught, we "cannot serve God and mammon" (Matt. 6:24). We cannot truly love God if we love our possessions, for then we will serve mammon instead.

Basil was a myrrhbearer, but he was also a pioneer, for he created the glorious, bustling, loving Basiliad, where he and those he trained showed genuine love to lepers and the disabled, to the hungry and the sick. The way he embraced people, teaching those who served there to think of the poor and infirm as their own brothers and sisters, tells us that this was truly a holy place. The poor who came to Basiliad may have been hungry for food, but surely they also hungered for love and companionship. Basil understood the importance of both.

As a shepherd and bishop, Basil was a myrrhbearer to more than the poor and the infirm. By inviting the wealthy people of his community to fund Basiliad and to work there, interacting with people and taking care of them, he gave the rich an opportunity to grow in love and to be transformed. He saw how they suffered spiritually, their souls prevented from soaring because they were tied down to their possessions and their wealth. He was trying to free them so that they could serve God by serving their neighbors, and he offered an example and ample opportunities, as well as plenty of sermons to encourage them in their efforts.

Basil cared both for those in danger of starvation and for those in spiritual peril because of their preoccupation with preserving wealth. With one grand, ambitious project, he undertook to care for all—rich and poor—and he set an example for the ages.

FOR REFLECTION

- Like so many monastics, Basil was challenged by Christ's words to the rich man to sell all he owned (Matt. 19:16–22). Basil heard a call in his heart: He knew that to be perfected, he would have to give everything away. Do you think that Christ intends that literally for all of us? Are we all called to poverty?

- Basil would have preferred to live in the wilderness forever, but he was called back to serve as a bishop. Had he never answered that call, so many of his truly valuable accomplishments would not have happened. Have you ever put your own desires aside to accept God's will for your life? What kind of fruit has that borne?

- Can you imagine a modern-day Basiliad? What would it be like?

JOHN THE MERCIFUL

Saint John the Merciful (or the Almsgiver, if you prefer)[1] was born to Prince Epiphanius and his wife on the island of Cyprus in the seventh century. He was raised as a Christian, and in his youth he had a vision that would forever impact his life: The beautiful maiden Compassion, crowned with a garland of olives, told John that she was the eldest daughter of the Great King. John was so moved by this vision that he dedicated his life to serving God by embracing compassion.

Under pressure from his parents, John married and had children, but both his wife and his children passed away. Enduring this great grief seems only to have made him ever more compassionate and faithful.

In the time of Emperor Heraclius, the widower John was chosen to serve as the Patriarch of Alexandria. He was known for piety and compassion, and now that his position provided a greater opportunity to show love, he took advantage of it. He ordered his stewards to compile a list of every poor and downtrodden person in Alexandria, and he collected their names—more than seven thousand of them—thinking of each one as an individual rather than simply seeing needy masses before him. John declared that he

---

1   From the account in *The Prologue of Ohrid*, November 12, 1. St. John the Merciful, Patriarch of Alexandria, and at https://www.oca.org/saints/live for November 12, Saint John the Merciful, Patriarch of Alexandria.

would watch over them and insisted that the Church's funds take care of them. John would call the poor his "Lords and Masters," explaining that they would have great influence at the Last Judgment. He would not turn away anyone in need.

John was an excellent patriarch and truly a humble servant. At one point, in the midst of serving the Divine Liturgy, his conscience was pricked: One of the clerics there at the cathedral had done something wrong, and John had scolded him. Now the man was angry with him, and St. John thought of our Lord's admonition: "Therefore if you bring your gift to the altar, and there remember that your brother has something against you, leave your gift there before the altar, and go your way. First be reconciled to your brother, and then come and offer your gift" (Matt. 5:23–24).

With no concern for appearances, the patriarch left the Holy Gifts at the altar and made his way over to the cleric. In full view of the entire congregation, he fell down in prostration before him, pleading for forgiveness. He would not return to the oblation until he knew that he was at peace with his brother. The cleric forgave him, and seeing this beautiful example, repented of his sin and changed his ways.

An Attentive Shepherd

Every Wednesday and Friday, Patriarch John came out from the cathedral and in the simplest and clearest way showed that he truly was there to shepherd every member of his flock: He sat on the church portico to receive anyone who wished to speak to him. This time was like "office hours" today—an open opportunity for any person to approach the patriarch with his needs. He patiently listened for hours. He settled quarrels, helped the wronged, and distributed alms.

With a patriarch so openly interested in almsgiving, it is no surprise that people occasionally tried to take advantage of the situation. Sometimes, a person who had no real need of help would come and apply for assistance, falsifying their poverty in order to swindle the Church out of some funds. Once, when Patriarch John was visiting the sick, a homeless man appeared and asked for alms. The patriarch asked that he be given six silver coins. A few moments later, having changed his clothes and run ahead, the same man appeared before the patriarch, asking for alms. Again Patriarch John granted him six silver coins. When he showed up a third time asking for alms, the servants accompanying the patriarch began to grumble and to chase him away—but the patriarch stopped them, ordering them to give him twelve pieces of silver, saying, "Perhaps he is Christ putting me to the test."

Another time, the patriarch was on his way to the Church of Saints Cyrus and John, and he came across a widow in need. She had an unfortunate tale and wanted to tell him everything. The patriarch listened closely and nodded his head, taking in every detail of her misfortune. The clergy who were escorting him began to lose patience as the woman droned on and on. Finally, they urged him to leave her and to hurry over to the church for the service; after all, they didn't want him to be late! They suggested that perhaps he could hear the rest of her tale at a more convenient time. Patriarch John simply replied, "And how will God listen to me, if I do not listen to her?" The group was silenced and stood patiently, as John remained with her, letting her talk until she was satisfied.

This kind of generosity with his time and attention is another kind of mercy he perfected as he strove to show compassion in all things. It isn't easy to put our own agenda and schedule aside to focus on someone God has placed in our path. We can see in

John's answer how he managed it: Just as Christ identified Himself with the poor and hungry ("for I was hungry and you gave Me food" [Matt. 25:35]), John identified himself with the unfortunate widow, allowing him to draw on an endless reserve of patience and compassion. For we all have patience with ourselves, and if we can love our neighbor as ourselves, we can tap into that infinite reserve!

Patriarch John was merciful in every way—generous with alms and quick to forgive, patient and compassionate. He was also a strict ascetic and a man of constant prayer. He was always mindful of his soul and even ordered that a coffin be made for him but left incomplete. He asked the carpenter to come to his cathedral on every feast day to inquire whether it was time to finish it yet, and in this way St. John was reminded that his end was near. This mindfulness of death kept him humble and seeking to live as if Christ's return was imminent: For suddenly the Judge shall come, and He may even be standing here now, in the form of the beggar before us.

FOR REFLECTION

- John showed mercy in a number of ways: through generosity, through a lack of judgment and condemnation, and through patience and compassion. Which of these are you best at practicing, and which is the hardest for you? Why?

- John had a few habitual ways of thinking that helped him maintain his high level of mercy:

  - He reminded himself that every beggar, no matter how dishonest or strange, could be Christ testing him.

  - He identified personally with those who sought him, asking how he could ever demand God's attention if he wouldn't pay attention to the person before him.

  - He reminded himself that death is always around the corner, and with it, the dread judgment seat of Christ.

- Which of these ways of thinking might you implement in order to live more mercifully?

COSMAS AND DAMIAN

A certain class of saints is known as the holy unmercenaries because they worked as doctors and healers, serving people of every economic group and social rank without accepting a fee for their work. They lived according to our Lord's command:

> "Heal the sick, cleanse the lepers, raise the dead, cast out demons. Freely you have received, freely give. Provide neither gold nor silver nor copper in your money belts, nor bag for *your* journey, nor two tunics, nor sandals, nor staffs; for a worker is worthy of his food." (Matt. 10:8–10)

Among the greatest of the holy unmercenaries is a pair of twin brothers, Cosmas and Damian, for whom the question of payment became a source of strife and division. Nonetheless, they are among the most beloved of the unmercenaries.[1] Born in the third century somewhere in Asia Minor or possibly in Mesopotamia, their pagan father died when they were still very young, and they were raised by their widowed Christian mother, Theodota. She educated the boys well and invited God to help her raise them,

---

1   Based on the account in *The Prologue of Ohrid*, November 1, "Saints Cosmas and Damian," and on the biography at https://www.oca.org/saints/live for November 1, "Holy Wonderworkers and Unmercenaries Cosmas and Damian of Mesopotamia."

and He did. God bestowed His grace on their little family, and Cosmas and Damian matured into devoted Christians. Trained and skilled as physicians, the Holy Spirit granted them the gift of healing people's illnesses of body and soul by the power of prayer.

Voluntary Poverty

Their ability to heal was in every way a gift from God, and so the brothers made a pact never to accept payment for their work. In this way, they honored God and His generosity while also ensuring a more ascetic lifestyle through their chosen poverty. They healed anyone and everyone for free, whether they needed physical or spiritual care or, as was most common, both. On occasion, they even healed animals—they were happy to serve in even the humblest of circumstances. At a time when medicine offered little relief, true healers were both a great marvel and a tremendous comfort, and their fame began to spread throughout the surrounding region.

According to Patriarch Pavle of Serbia in his sermon on these unmercenary brothers,

> As Christians, they healed people both with medicines, the knowledge they had acquired, but also with their humane, Christian, brotherly approach toward the sick, toward people who are in distress—those whose circumstances were truly most difficult, and who needed both a humane word, as well as human, brotherly help.[2]

---

2   Patriarch Pavle of Serbia and H. Middleton, *Life According to the Gospel*, Contemporary Christian Thought Series, no. 37 (Sebastian Press, 2017), 163.

The healing they offered was more than medicine: It was augmented with love and compassion. So often, when we think of human needs, we consider the basics: food, shelter, medical care. Social needs, however, are every bit as important; in fact, recent studies suggest "that the magnitude of the effect of social isolation on mortality risk may be comparable to or greater than other well-established risk factors such as smoking, obesity, and physical inactivity."[3] Loneliness is a health concern and threatens our longevity like the more obvious health risks. Cosmas and Damian—and Christian caregivers in general—focus on both the care itself and the love and compassion that must accompany it, bringing both medical knowledge and companionship to their patients.

Cosmas and Damian did not work alone, for the love they brought to their patients was actually the love of God. As Patriarch Pavle puts it, they were collaborating with God:

In this world, struggles, sicknesses, and misfortune are unavoidable. However, you know that we are all assistants, collaborators of God in the act of the preservation of our life and our health both with regard to medical treatment, but also with regard to the act of our salvation. Let us do what we can as coworkers of God; anything more than what our time and circumstances demand of us will be done by Him.[4]

The brothers were co-laboring with God; filled with the Holy Spirit, their work was a synergy of divine and human efforts. Doctors working alone cannot offer salvation, but where God is part

---

3   See National Academies of Sciences, Engineering, and Medicine, "Social Isolation and Loneliness in Older Adults: Opportunities for the Health Care System" (The National Academies Press, 2020), https://doi .org/10.17226/25663.

4   Patriarch Pavle, 163.

of the work, the healing is salvific. These twin doctors engaged in the highest kind of myrrhbearing: the work of both God and man, a collaborative effort whose efficacy knew no bounds. Because of their love for God and for their neighbors, and because of their holy and pure hearts, they were able to manifest divine love in the healing of souls and bodies.

A Break in Communion

But a disagreement interrupted their wonderful ministry. At one point, a terribly sick woman named Palladia approached the brothers. Convinced her case was hopeless, her doctors had simply given up on her. The brothers likewise had no medicine that would address her illness, so they relied on God for a miracle, fervently praying that He would have mercy on her. Through their prayers, God acted: Palladia rose from her bed healed, and she was beside herself with gratitude for this second chance at life. She was so delighted that when she next saw Damian, she presented him with three eggs and said, "Take this small gift in the Name of the Holy Life-Creating Trinity, the Father, Son, and Holy Spirit."[5]

Damian was stuck: He and his brother had agreed never to accept payment for any healing. And yet, here stood this woman, grateful to God and to the brothers for their intercessions, hoping to make a small offering in return. How would she feel if Damian refused the eggs? Might she feel shamed, as if she had been corrected or scolded? Is it more gracious to accept a gift than to refuse it?

---

5   From the https://www.oca.org/saints/live article for November 1, "Holy Wonderworkers and Unmercenaries Cosmas and Damian of Mesopotamia."

Palladia understood that the brothers were unmercenary, and so she did not offer silver or gold but instead offered simple, inexpensive eggs, like those a humble farmer might put on his own table. In ancient times when one had an audience with the emperor, it was customary to present him with a gift. Impoverished people would give a small, symbolic gift, as Mary Magdalen did when she presented Emperor Tiberius with an egg. Similarly, Palladia was honoring the brothers with a symbolic offering of three eggs—not enough to be a worthy payment for their work, but something that would express her love and profound gratitude for their prayers. She chose three eggs, in honor of the Holy Trinity. Hearing the Father, Son, and Holy Spirit named, the unmercenary Damian did not dare to refuse. He accepted the eggs, which we can imagine gratified Palladia and brought her joy.

When his brother, Cosmas, learned that Damian accepted the eggs, he grew very sad, for the vow was broken: Damian was no longer a pure unmercenary. Leaving no room for *economia* or mercy, Cosmas believed that the rule they agreed to was very clear, with no possible exceptions. On his deathbed, Cosmas gave instructions that his brother should not be buried beside him. Having broken a lifetime of communion with his twin, he died in estrangement. Though he spent his whole life serving others with love and compassion, at his death he showed no mercy to either Palladia or to his own twin brother.

Patriarch Pavle addressed the urge to correct our brother when he sins. He agrees that it can be necessary to help save his soul, but he also quotes Basil the Great as having said, "Do not be a fratricide on account of false brotherly love." He writes, "When we condemn our brother, we do not exalt ourselves with actual effort to be lifted up, morally and spiritually; rather, we push him down, so that the distance between us is to his detriment, and so that we can appear in the eyes of the world as higher and better than him."[6]

Surely Cosmas did not intend to exalt himself in the eyes of those present, but he did pronounce a very public and permanent memorial to what he saw as his brother's ruin when he demanded that they be buried separately. The memorials that marked their separate graves could not help but commemorate their obvious separation and the punishment he inflicted on Damian.

The Desert Fathers taught a very different way to handle our brother's sins: "A certain brother also asked [him], 'If I see my brother committing a fault, is it good to conceal it?' And the geronda said, 'Whenever we overlook a brother's fault, God overlooks our own. And whenever we proclaim our brother's faults, God likewise proclaims ours.'"[7]

A Gift of Clarity

And indeed, God did make a proclamation. Soon after Cosmas's death, Damian also died, and there was debate about where to bury him. Should they obey Cosmas's wishes and take Damian somewhere else? Where would they go? And was it right to honor such a wish? Soon God intervened with a miracle to set the situation right. A camel the brothers had tamed spoke to the crowd, saying quite clearly that there should be no doubt: Damian did not accept the eggs from the woman as payment for services rendered but out of respect for the Name of God. Damian should be buried beside his brother because he did not break his vow, and he remained unmercenary to the end. The camel's miraculous words acquitted Damian and confirmed that his merciful exception had

---

6   Patriarch Pavle, 111.
7   Benedicta Ward, ed., "Judgmentalism," *The Sayings of the Desert Fathers: The Alphabetical Collection*, vol. 6 (Cistercian Publications, 1984), 100.

no mercenary motivation. The beast also implicitly proclaimed Cosmas's sin of judgment and condemnation. The brothers were buried together at Thereman in Mesopotamia.

The story of Cosmas and Damian is a true myrrhbearing tale. The brothers humbly and selflessly offered the gifts they received from God and looked only for His blessings in return. Their myrrhbearing was a literal caretaking of human bodies as well as those of animals. Because they worked in synergy with God, they were able to provide to the people they encountered not just their medical expertise, but also spiritual guidance and miraculous healings of soul and body. When two people gather to work together in Christ's name, putting their own comfort and ambition aside and working instead to fulfill God's will, they can make a tremendous impact on our broken and suffering world.

Cosmas and Damian, as well as the camel they healed, reveal another important aspect of myrrhbearing: True love and service must always be offered with mercy. When we judge our brothers, we break communion; we commit fratricide in the name of brotherly love. God's voice—even through a camel—brings us into unity, as it is always His will that we walk together in loving communion.

FOR REFLECTION

- We have seen that the brothers co-labored with God. Is this a possibility for all of us? How might we achieve such synergy?

- When we take a vow before God, or perhaps embark on a Lenten period, we hope to fulfill it without exception. Yet this story asks how fastidious we should be when dealing with other people. Is it possible that in some ways, it is unmerciful to be *perfectly* unmercenary? Is perfectionism itself a problem?

- How do we discern when we should hold to the rule and when we should grant a merciful exception?

RIGHTEOUS JOSEPH
THE PATRIARCH

Joseph may be best remembered as the son whose loving father gave him a coat of many colors, igniting his brothers' envy, but there is much more to the story of one of history's greatest myrrhbearers.[1] Like Christ, Joseph was righteous and patient; he endured betrayal and affliction prayerfully, in silence. The Fathers of the Church understand Joseph as a type of Christ, as his story foreshadows much of our Lord's own story:[2]

> As a figure of the Lord, O my soul, the righteous and gentle Joseph was sold into bondage by his brethren; but thou hast sold thyself entirely to thy sins.
>
> O miserable and wicked soul, imitate the righteous and pure mind of Joseph. . . .

---

1   Biographical information comes from Genesis 37—50.
2   Both Joseph and Jesus are the most beloved sons of their fathers, and both are innocent men, betrayed (one for twenty and the other for thirty pieces of silver) and then stripped and cast into darkness (a pit and the Pit, as Hades is known in the Psalms); both were thought to be dead but indeed are alive. Prophecies say that people will bow down before them, and each of them will save their people, Israel, delivering them from death.

Once Joseph was cast into a pit, O Lord and Master, as a figure of Thy burial and resurrection. But what offering such as this shall I ever make to Thee? [3]

Joseph's brothers took his coat of many colors—the symbol of his favored status in their father's eyes—and threw him into a pit, then sold him to a group of passing Midianite traders, who carried him far away to Egypt. Pharaoh's captain of the guard, Potiphar, purchased Joseph, and Joseph began a new chapter as a servant in Egypt. Potiphar's wife framed Joseph for rape and had him thrown into prison, but he remained prayerful and uncomplaining. In response, God continued to bless him. By granting him miraculous insight into the meaning of dreams, He delivered Joseph from prison, elevating him to overseer of Pharaoh's house and, eventually, of all that he had. Joseph's situation was terrible—betrayal, slavery, slander, prison—until suddenly it was very good—freedom, promotion, power, and riches. But Joseph's goodness and faith never wavered. His humility was so great that he was not offended by the bad, and he was not flattered by the good.

Myrrhbearing on a Grand Scale

God revealed to Joseph the meaning of Pharaoh's mysterious dreams: There would be seven years of plenty and then seven years of famine. Pharaoh recognized "the Spirit of God" (Gen. 41:38) in Joseph, so he entrusted Joseph to steward Egypt. He did so skillfully, enforcing moderation in the fat years, saving up excess grain for the coming famine. The Scriptures say that Joseph "went throughout all the land of Egypt" (Gen. 41:46) and that he

---

3   Canticle Five from the Great Compline for Monday of the first week of Great Lent, *The Lenten Triodion*, 203–4.

"gathered very much grain, as the sand of the sea, until he stopped counting, for *it was* immeasurable" (Gen. 41:49). He did not become the sort of ruler who sits in the palace and gives orders but instead emptied himself out with hard work to prevent the great tragedy that loomed on the horizon. This was a myrrhbearing act on a grand scale.

Genesis 41 continues:

> Then the seven years of plenty in the land of Egypt ended, and the seven years of famine began to come, as Joseph said. The famine was in all lands, but in all the land of Egypt there was bread. So when all the land of Egypt was famished, the people cried to Pharaoh for bread. Then Pharaoh said to all the Egyptians, "Go to Joseph; whatever he says to you, do." The famine was over all the face of the earth, and Joseph opened all the storehouses and sold to the Egyptians. Then all countries also came to Joseph in Egypt to buy *grain*, because the famine was severe in all the earth. (vv. 53–57)

When this terrible famine arrived, Joseph's hard work paid off, and he saved thousands of people from starvation. He nourished all of Egypt and then people from other lands. Joseph literally saved the known world from severe famine.

People came from everywhere—including Joseph's own homeland, the land of Canaan. Jacob sent Joseph's brothers to buy grain in Egypt, and when they arrived, Joseph recognized them immediately. But they did not recognize him—they would never have expected to see their brother as the savior and ruler of Egypt. At no point does Joseph ever lash out or attempt to avenge himself. Instead, like the father who saw his prodigal son coming up the road (Luke 15:11–32), Joseph slaughtered a fatted calf and set up a banquet—in a time of great famine—where he and his brothers could break bread and begin to restore the communion of their broken family.

The conversation turned to Jacob and his profound grief at the loss of his son Joseph. It was all too much for Joseph—he could no longer restrain his emotions, and so he finally revealed himself:

> Then he said: "I am Joseph your brother, whom you sold into Egypt. But now, do not therefore be grieved or angry with yourselves because you sold me here; for God sent me before you to preserve life. For these two years the famine has been in the land, and there are still five years in which there will be neither plowing nor harvesting. And God sent me before you to preserve a posterity for you in the earth, and to save your lives by a great deliverance. So now it was not you who sent me here, but God; and He has made me a father to Pharaoh, and lord of all his house, and a ruler throughout all the land of Egypt. (Gen. 45:4–8)

Restoration

Joseph forgave his brothers and even asked them to forgive themselves! He saw God's hand in all of this; it was Providence that allowed him to be sold away to Egypt, for God took care of him every step of the way. Saint John Chrysostom observes,

> That servitude, Joseph is saying, procured for me this position. That sale brought me to this prominence. That distress proved the occasion of this honor for me. That envy produced this glory for me. Let us not simply hear this but also emulate it. In the same way let us comfort those badly disposed to us, relieving them of responsibility for what has been done to us and putting up with everything with great equanimity, like this remarkable man.[4]

---

4   Chrysostom, "Homily 46" on the Gospel of John.

Not only did Joseph resist holding on to understandable anger and resentment, but he embraced his brothers with love and generosity—he entered back into communion with his family. So many of us would be reluctant to give up the powerful feeling of having been wronged; after all, being the injured party places us in a morally superior position to our attackers. Joseph was humble enough to freely release that power over them and to replace negative feelings with positivity, creating room for a fresh, new beginning.

In a beautiful fifth-century sermon, St. Caesarius, bishop of Arles, talked about Joseph's attitude:

> He did not recall that pit into which he had been thrown to be murdered; he did not think of himself, a brother, sold for a price. Instead, by returning good for evil, even then he fulfilled the precepts of the apostles that were not yet given. Therefore, by considering the sweetness of true charity, blessed Joseph, with God's help, was eager to repel from his heart the poison of envy with which he knew his brothers had been struck.[5]

Joseph could have focused on those elements of his life that would stir up anger, resentment, and envy. Instead, as Paul exhorts us in Philippians 4:8, he meditated on "whatever things *are* true, whatever things *are* noble, whatever things *are* just, whatever things *are* pure, whatever things *are* lovely, whatever things *are* of good report," turning to thoughts of "virtue" and "anything praiseworthy." Filled with love for God, Joseph saw only ways to make love grow and to fulfill all righteousness.

---

5   St. Caesarius of Arles, *St. Caesarius Sermons Volume II (81–186)*, trans. Sr. Mary Magdaleine Mueller, The Fathers of the Church Patristic Series, vol. 47 (Catholic University of America Press, 2010), 46.

Envy was the root of the sin his brothers committed against him. Had Joseph sunk into envy because his cruel brothers continued to live in the home he so dearly missed, the envy that took them down would have taken him as well. Instead, with his eyes on God and his hands dedicated to service, Joseph simply multiplied his blessings, again and again.

"I Belong to God"

If there is any doubt about Joseph's reason for forgiving his brothers, he clarifies it at the very end of the Book of Genesis:

> So Joseph said to them, "Do not be afraid, for I belong to God. But as for you, you meant evil against me; but God meant it for good, in order to bring it about as it is this day, to save many people alive. Now therefore, do not be afraid; I will provide for you and your households." Thus he comforted them and spoke to their heart. (Gen. 50:19–21 [OSB])

If we wish to follow Joseph's example, we can locate the heart of his attitude in this one phrase: "for I belong to God." This understanding operates on many levels. Joseph knew that nothing could befall him that God did not allow. At every turn of fortune, Joseph knew that he belonged to God, a statement that also implies its corollary: God considered Joseph one of His own; He valued him, watched over him, and loved him. Because Joseph trusted God so much, he was comforted in every difficulty. He was not blind to the fact that his brothers intended evil for him, but because "God meant it for good," his circumstance was good.

God means everything for good, always. God is all goodness; God is love. Many centuries later, St. Paul affirmed this truth in his Letter to the Romans: "And we know that all things work together for good to those who love God, to those who are the called according to *His* purpose" (8:28). Evil intentions may cause our misfortunes, but when we understand that we belong to God, all things are transformed.

Deliverance and Communion

Joseph told his brothers to bring his father, Jacob, and all that they owned back to Egypt, to live near him in the land of Goshen, where he would take care of them (Gen. 45:10–11). Joseph provided more than wheat to keep his family alive; he gave them a new home. When they arrived, like the father of the prodigal son "he fell on his brother Benjamin's neck and wept," then "he kissed all his brothers and wept over them, and after this his brothers talked with him" (Gen. 45:14–15). This physical and emotional reconnection restored the communion of this great family; after the embraces came conversation—they were brothers again. Joseph saved his family from brokenness, and he saved God's people, the nation that would bear messianic fruit.

The brothers brought Jacob to Goshen, and the family settled in this new location. They had been delivered from famine, and Egypt became their safe haven. Jacob lived out his final years with all his sons restored to him in a harmony they had not known before. And when this great patriarch died, Joseph and his brothers honored his dying wish to be buried with his fathers in the cave where Abraham and Sarah, Isaac, Rebekah, and Leah were buried. Jacob was embalmed and mourned by Egypt for seventy days, then the entire family joined in a great procession of Egyptians, chariots, and horses with Jacob's body (Gen. 50:7–11). Beyond the Jordan, the people mourned in a solemn, seven-day spectacle that caused the local inhabitants to rename the place as "the Mourning of Egypt."

Joseph became a literal myrrhbearer for Jacob, having him embalmed and handling complex funeral arrangements to honor him. But he had already shown himself to be a myrrhbearer as he emptied himself out to store up food and then compassionately nourished the known world through severe famine. Joseph rejected and reversed powerful envy, refusing this ugly emotion any harbor in his own soul; he purged his family of the great sin that plagued his own fortunes. If envy, that hatred of other people's good fortune and blessings, is the enemy of myrrhbearing, then Joseph is the great champion and defender of myrrhbearing itself, for he defeated envy and, through his love for God, allowed glorious communion to burst forth and multiply.

FOR REFLECTION

- If ever a person had a "right" to be angry and resentful, it was Joseph. Are our "rights" always compatible with our joy?

- If no matter what evil befalls us, "God meant it for good" and ultimately it results in good, what power does evil have?

- Does this way of living and seeing the world seem too much to you? Christ once asked, "Do you want to be made well?" (John 5:6). Do you want to follow Joseph's example, if it leads to such abundant joy?

STYLIANOS

Stylianos was born in the fifth century, in the province of Paphlagonia in Asia Minor.[1] He was a devout Christian from birth, and when he came of age, he chose to give away all his possessions—an act that he would refer to as "casting off a heavy anchor." Like so many ascetic Christians, Stylianos found that the responsibilities and temptations associated with possessing property, objects, and wealth interrupted his ability to "see more plainly the road to real life," the life in Christ.

Seeking God

Stylianos became a monk and earnestly dedicated himself to repentance—to a constant turning toward God. His days were filled with prayer and service, and yet he hungered for more. He decided to leave the monastery and head for the desert to live in a cave out in the wilderness. This lifestyle brought him great joy and peace. In the quiet of the desert, he contemplated God and His creation. He

---

1 Based on the account in *The Prologue of Ohrid*, November 26, and on the blog post by Archimandrite Haralambos D. Vasilopoulos, "Saint Stylianos, the Protector of Children," *Orthodox Youth Resources*, November 26, 2019, https://www.orthodoxyouthresources.com/2019/11/saint-stylianos-protector-of-children.html.

cried out with the psalmist, "How magnificent are your works, O Lord" (Ps. 91:6/92:5)! and offered praise and worship.

Unlike many other ascetics, however, Stylianos did not live entirely as a hermit but would venture occasionally among people. He was called to community, it seems. But for several decades, Stylianos lived primarily in the desert, struggling against temptations and giving himself more fully to God. God rewarded his efforts and, in time, transformed him. He radiated God's light, and before long, people were drawn to him. Stylianos was a joyful man with a bright smile for every visitor, and he was happy to share wisdom and loving words of advice. He knew how to calm troubled souls. Pilgrims traveled to the wilderness to find the monk and spend time with him, and many of them found their lives forever altered by the experience.

Tradition holds that one night as Stylianos was deep in prayer, seeking God's guidance on how best to help those who came to him, he felt a divine presence, as if he were consumed by the great glory of the Holy Spirit. The next morning, when he emerged from his cave, he was filled with a joy and serenity he never had known before. As usual, he received his visitors and spoke words of encouragement and wisdom, but for the first time he felt compelled to place his hand on the head of a sick child whose mother had brought him to the desert for the monk's prayers. As he touched the child, he felt the power of God moving through him, and the child immediately recovered. Word spread, and more parents brought their ailing children.

Because he lived out in the wilderness, it wasn't easy to seek healing miracles from Stylianos. Mothers walked for miles, their sick children in their arms or across their shoulders, until they came to his tiny cell. Again and again, they offered up children in various states of distress, and Stylianos tirelessly tended to them. He would approach the child with love and compassion and begin to pray. Time after time, through his fervent prayers and through the presence of the Holy Spirit within him, God would heal their sickness.

Sometimes women who yearned to be mothers but had not conceived, or who could not carry a child to term, would come to Stylianos. He would pray over them, and the prayers were answered, for they conceived and gave birth to healthy babies. Stylianos became renowned for working miracles for children—for those who were gravely ill, or for those whose yearning mothers were granted their dearest wish.

As his fame spread, Stylianos was approached not only by the faithful needing healing and assistance, but also at times by greedy mercenaries who presented a variety of business propositions for the monk. They wanted to commercialize his talents, selling miraculous healings for a small fortune. Stylianos always had the same answer for them: He had been paid in advance for his services when the Holy Spirit, with the peace which surpasses understanding, came upon him. He needed nothing more. As they left, disappointed, his face would shine with his customary smile.

A New Ministry Unfolds

Stylianos had withdrawn from society and found that he loved living alone with God in the wilderness—and yet, a new chapter in his life was opening. He was finding great joy in his healing ministries. Stylianos felt called to return to the city so that he might live closer to the people he loved to serve. In this new location, it was much easier for parents to bring their sick children to him. The smiling monk always received them warmly. In time, he began to take in orphans, and soon parents began to entrust him with their children's care and education. While they were busy at work, Stylianos would watch over their boys and girls, instilling in them the radiant love of God. Stylianos founded what many call the world's first day care center. He watched over so many children that he had to recruit other monks to come join him, and this holy group spent their days tending to the needs of God's most innocent and beloved creations. They fed and consoled the little ones, prayed with them and taught them, and poured love and compassion on them. Their practical and loving service for the least of these was true myrrhbearing work.

Stylianos's time in the wilderness had brought him great joy, giving him the space he needed to die to his passions so that desires for things like comfort and food and even community had no more power over him. He was completely free to love God, and the fruits of his prayers were visible to all: He radiated Christ's love. He became a wonderworker, and the power of God flowed through his fingertips. God granted him the gift of being a healing myrrhbearer, and as he leaned into this transformation, Stylianos emerged from the wilderness to provide real, daily care—physical and spiritual—for children.

The day care center of the desert monastics must have been a fascinating place. It would be wonderful to learn what became of the children who grew up in the arms of these spiritual giants who had humility enough to come and serve the babies while their mothers worked or took care of other needs. The mark of a true Christian is humility, so perhaps we should not be surprised that the holiest hermits were quick to heed Christ's call to serve the tiniest of His sheep.

Stylianos lived to be an old man, always surrounded by babies and children. He was a myrrhbearer and a wonderworker to the end, blessing all who came to him with his joyful smile, prayers, and—of course—miraculous healings. It is said that when he died, his countenance radiated the light of God, and his eyes were filled with great joy; he died with his customary smile on his face. In his icons, he stands with a baby in his arms, a testament to his loving, myrrhbearing work.

FOR REFLECTION

- Like so many monastics, St. Stylianos went out to the desert, where alone in the wilderness he could come to know God, and only occasionally did he return to the city. If solitude in the desert was necessary for him to become so holy, why do you suppose the noise of the city did not dampen his holiness on his return?

- How do you think St. Stylianos discerned that his calling was specific to helping children, as well as helping women who yearned to bear children? Could this apply to how you might discern your calling?

- Christ teaches that we must become like children to enter the Kingdom (Matt. 18:1–5). What is it in children that He calls us to emulate, and how can we do that?

JOHN MAXIMOVITCH

In 1896, a frail, sickly, and bookish young man named Michael was born in Ukraine.[1] His family were very pious aristocrats—they attended church regularly and took Michael on pilgrimages to visit holy icons and relics. As he got older, his parents sent him to military school, after which he earned a law degree in 1918. The family fled their homeland as the Bolshevik revolutionaries spread to Ukraine.

The Maximovitch family evacuated to Yugoslavia, where Michael got another degree, this time in theology. All in one year (1926), he was tonsured a monk, given the name John, and ordained a hierodeacon then a hieromonk. He was teaching in a Serbian high school and serving in a local parish. The people there loved him, and soon the bishops of the Russian Church Abroad decided to elevate him to the episcopate.

John was very humble, so he was skeptical when he was called to Belgrade to talk about being elevated to bishop. On the streetcar, as he headed to the meeting, he told someone that he'd been accidentally summoned—they were hoping to elevate another monk named John and had mistakenly written to him. The next day, he happened across that same woman and told her that their mistake

---

1 Biographical information is based on the account, "The Life of St. John Maximovich, Founder of our Parish" at https://stjohndc.org/en/our-parish /our-history/life-stjohn-maximovich-founder-our-parish.

was far worse than he thought: They really did want to make him a bishop!

After his elevation, Bishop John was sent to Shanghai to watch over a large community who fled the Soviet Union, finding shelter in China. He was truly a good shepherd, kind and tender with his flock. The Russians call their bishops *Vladyka*, and Vladyka John was deeply loved by his people. Though his position justified some pomp and circumstance, John wore clothing made from cheap materials and walked around barefoot. Indeed, when people insisted that he wear shoes, he played with them a bit: The Russian word for "wear" is the same as the word for "carry," so in response, he would tuck his shoes under his arm and carry them cheerfully.

Shanghai

Vladyka John loved children, and as a true myrrhbearer, he loved "the least of these": He had a very tender heart for orphans. When he arrived in Shanghai, he found eight orphans there, so he immediately started an orphanage. He encouraged the ladies from his parish to form a committee, rent a house, and create a home for orphans and children whose parents were impoverished. Over three thousand children would pass through the orphanage—and every one of them had a traumatic story.

For example, a boy named Paul was an eyewitness to the murder of his father and mother by the Communists. The trauma left him mute and wild—like a trapped animal, he was afraid of everyone and was always fighting and spitting. The ladies were reluctant to bring him into the already overcrowded orphanage, lest he hurt the other children. When Vladyka John heard about this boy, he dropped everything to visit him. He told the boy, "I know that you have lost your father, but now you have found another one—me," and embraced him. The boy burst into tears, and his speech returned to him.

At that time China was war-torn, and Chinese families had many children and very little food. Sometimes, they would find that they could not afford another child, or they discovered that their newborn had a defect, like a club foot or a cleft lip and palate. In those cases, the babies were sometimes left outside to freeze to death. Thank God, Vladyka John was able to intervene in many cases. He would walk the Shanghai streets at night, listening for the cries of abandoned babies. When he found them, he carried them home to the orphanage.

One woman, Mrs. Shakhmatova, had the opportunity to see how Vladyka worked. He asked her to buy two bottles of Chinese vodka—which seemed odd to her, but she did it—and then invited her to walk with him into some very dangerous neighborhoods at night. As they walked, she saw drunk people and dangerous-looking characters everywhere. Then they heard a growl. It came from a drunken man who was seated in a dark doorway, and they could hear the faint moan of a baby in a nearby garbage can. When Vladyka moved toward the baby, the drunk man growled again as if to warn him to stay back. Vladyka John calmly turned to Mrs. Shakhmatova, saying quietly, "Hand me a bottle." He held out the bottle in one hand and pointed to the garbage can with the other—silently offering a trade. Vladyka walked away with the baby girl in his arms. That same night, he found another little girl and returned to the orphanage with two babies in his arms.

Every day Vladyka John visited the sick and the infirm, praying for them and offering whatever assistance he could. At one point, he went to the hospital to see a young man who had been diagnosed with just a short time to live. Vladyka walked into the room and saw him as well as his roommate in the next bed—a talkative, energetic young man who was very happy that he was being discharged and would go home the next morning. Vladyka John immediately focused on the energetic patient, insisting that he must receive Holy Communion. He was happy to comply. He made his confession and received communion, and Vladyka left. One of the people followed him into the hall, asking why he hadn't visited at all with the dying man he'd been called to see. Vladyka answered that they had it all wrong—the sickly man would live many years, but the energetic one would die that night. He was right.

Saint John the Barefoot

When Communism took hold of China and Christians were no longer welcome there, Vladyka John and the entire Russian Orthodox community left together, bringing along all the orphans Vladyka had gathered. They went to the Philippines, where they lived in a refugee camp on an island that constantly experienced typhoons. One only can imagine how terrifying it must be to weather a typhoon in a tent. Every night, Vladyka John tirelessly would walk the perimeter, praying and blessing the camp. For the entire two years and three months that the little Russian community lived at that camp, not a single typhoon came near the island. When he was able, Vladyka moved his people—including every last orphan—into safe homes in Australia and the United States. Just two months after they left, a typhoon flattened the camp.

After the Philippines, Vladyka John was assigned to oversee the Russian Church in Western Europe, where the French gave him a new nickname: St. John the Barefoot, because he dressed so humbly and wore no shoes. He walked the streets tirelessly, moving from hospital to hospital to visit the sick.

Eventually, Vladyka John was reassigned to San Francisco, California. He worked to build a beautiful cathedral dedicated to a particular icon of the Mother of God known as the Joy of All Who Sorrow, with an attached orphanage and school. By this time, he had many spiritual children who came to him for confession or, if they lived far away, would write him letters. He was well known for reading and thoughtfully answering every single letter.[2]

From the time he was tonsured a monk, Vladyka John never lay down to sleep. He might doze in his chair for an hour or two here and there, but he would never lie down in a bed. He was tireless in his efforts to care for his beloved flock: Whether he was awake all night answering letters or out walking and praying for the city, he was always in service and never at rest. His myrrhbearing love was, and still is, literally inexhaustible.

---

2   Even now, long after his death, pilgrims leave letters for him in San Francisco's Holy Virgin Cathedral (Joy of All Who Sorrow) in a mail slot built into the case that holds his incorrupt relics.

FOR REFLECTION

- It's a very unusual circumstance for a bishop to be shepherding his people between countries, trying to find them safe harbor. Fleeing to a strange land must be incredibly scary and unsettling, and most refugees flee alone or as a family. How would it be different to experience this together as a parish community?

- Vladyka John's orphanage housed more than fifteen hundred children in his lifetime. How can we measure the impact of such a project?

- Vladyka John did not lie down, and he hardly slept. How do you suppose he continued to function so well? What benefit do you think he found in this arrangement?

NICHOLAS OF MYRA

S aint Nicholas the Wonderworker, the fourth-century arch-bishop of Myra in Lycia, is one of the most famous saints of all time.[1] He is a powerful intercessor, a speedy helper, and an extraordinary mediator before God. He is beloved around the world—largely because he's responsible for more miracles than any other, and in more places around the world. In the United States, we primarily know him as the model for Santa Claus, but that association does not do him justice. More than a giver of gifts, he was truly a saver of lives.

Even as a young man, Nicholas was devout and loved to study the Scriptures. His uncle, Bishop Nicholas of Patara, guided him and nurtured him in his faith. The bishop ordained his nephew a reader then elevated him to the priesthood. Though he was young, Nicholas was wise beyond his years, and the bishop made him his assistant and trusted him to instruct the flock. The young Fr. Nicholas made a wonderful impression on his community. He was vivacious, deeply prayerful, and showed amazing kindheartedness. He was good to the poor and the sick, and before long, he had dis-tributed his entire inheritance to the people in need around him.

---

[1] From the account at https://www.oca.org/saints/live, December 6, "Saint Nicholas the Wonderworker, Archbishop of Myra in Lycia," and the service, *Akathist and Life and Miracles of Saint Nicholas the Wonderworker* (Holy Trinity Monastery).

Quiet Charity

During these years, a wealthy man in Patara had three daughters and also a gambling problem. He lost everything. The daughters now faced a terrible predicament: Their dowries were gone, so they could not be given in proper marriages. Their father's solution was to consign them to a life of prostitution. Father Nicholas knew about the situation, and he acted discreetly to change the young women's fate: At night, he tossed a bag of gold coins, the amount of a respectable dowry, into the man's window. He received it, understood, and used it to give his eldest daughter in marriage. As each girl came of age, Fr. Nicholas tossed her dowry into the window at night. All three were saved—and their father was saved from committing far worse sins than he'd already indulged.[2]

Father Nicholas did not confront the man publicly, nor did he tell the daughters. Like the Virgin Mary at the wedding at Cana, he observed the situation and intervened quietly, before the town understood the problem. Father Nicholas was known both for his generosity and for always giving in secret and hiding his good deeds. He provided a living example of following our Lord's instructions:

> Take heed that you do not do your charitable deeds before men, to be seen by them. Otherwise you have no reward from your Father in heaven. Therefore, when you do a charitable deed, do not sound a trumpet before you as the hypocrites do in the synagogues and in the streets, that they may have glory from men. Assuredly, I say to you, they have their reward. But when you do a charitable deed, do not let your left hand know what your right

---

2   In some versions of the story, the gold coins land in the girls' stockings as they are hung on the mantle to dry—an explanation for why we hang stockings and receive gifts from Santa Claus.

hand is doing, that your charitable deed may be in secret; and your Father who sees in secret will Himself reward you openly. (Matt. 6:1–4)

Christ calls us to care for those in need, and our intentions matter: If we do good deeds in hope of receiving accolades, we will receive nothing more. On the other hand, if we do good deeds in secret, humbly and without drawing attention to ourselves, then we will receive rewards in heaven. Father Nicholas acted in secret because his intention was not to exalt himself but to serve others.

Father Nicholas took a pilgrimage to the Holy Land and visited Jerusalem—the Holy Sepulcher and Golgotha, Capernaum, Nazareth, Bethlehem, and all the holy places. He found a cave outside Bethlehem and spent some time there, living in the wilderness in the land where Jesus had lived.[3] He loved his time in the desert and considered settling there permanently, but a divine voice urged him to return home. Obediently, Nicholas headed for the city of Myra in Lycia.

The Bishop of Myra

Father Nicholas lived a quiet life in Myra until the local bishop fell asleep in the Lord. When the council met, the bishops decided to wait for God to reveal his successor. Soon, an elder bishop had a vision of Christ, who told him that the first man to enter the church for services that night would be named Nicholas, and he

---

3   At the Greek Orthodox Church of St. Nicholas in Beit Jala, Palestine, it is still possible to visit St. Nicholas's cave. When I visited there in 2019, I found it to be one of the holiest and most peaceful places I have ever been. The people in this parish tell amazing stories of very recent miracles worked by St. Nicholas out of his great love for the people of Beit Jala and his sympathy for the hardships they endure.

would become their new shepherd. Naturally, the bishops and the clergy flocked to the church to wait and see who would enter first! Father Nicholas, always the first to arrive, approached the door, but the elder bishop stopped him.

"What is your name?" he asked.

Father Nicholas responded, "My name is Nicholas, Master, and I am your servant."

Nicholas was elevated to become the bishop of Myra, and his flock loved him because he was a good shepherd: wise and gentle, firm and kind. Soon, Bishop Nicholas would be put to the test when Emperor Diocletian unleashed a great persecution on the Church in Myra. At one point, Bishop Nicholas and several other Christians were imprisoned. Behind bars, the bishop preached and reassured the other prisoners, giving them strength to reject false idols and to endure fetters, punishment, and torture in the name of Jesus Christ. With his encouragement, they stayed strong until the rise of Emperor Constantine and his issuance of the Edict of Milan in AD 313, which ended the persecutions and set the Christians free.

In 325, Emperor Constantine convened the First Ecumenical Council, gathering all the bishops and theologians, including Bishop Nicholas. At this council they would declare the Symbol of Faith (the Nicene Creed) and would denounce Arius, who taught that the Son of God was a created being, as a heretic. As they worked their way toward that conclusion, they debated Arius and his supporters. Bishop Nicholas was an excellent defender of the true Faith, and at one point he was so outraged at Arius's words that he yelled at him then hit him in the face. Due to this assault, he was placed under guard and was to be removed from the episcopacy—until several of the Fathers in the council had the same vision of Jesus and Mary the Mother of God returning the Gospel and omophorion to Nicholas. They all agreed that God did not wish to see Nicholas removed from the episcopate, and so he was restored to his position as bishop of Myra.

Back home, Bishop Nicholas brought peace and growth to his flock. He nourished them with sound doctrine, and when it was needed, he provided food for their bodies. They say that, just as Moses' face shone with God's glory (Ex. 34:29), the bishop's face was so filled with grace that sometimes the people who looked at him were astonished. During his life, several miracles happened through his prayers. For example, three men were unjustly condemned to death by the governor, who had been bribed. As the executioner stood with his sword raised, ready to chop off a head, Bishop Nicholas walked right up to him and took the sword from his hands. He denounced the governor for his wrongdoing, and the stunned governor repented and begged for forgiveness.

In another instance, a terrible famine hit, but the city of Myra was spared because the bishop appeared to an Italian merchant in his dreams and left him three real gold pieces as a pledge of payment. In this vision, the bishop ordered grain to be delivered to Myra, and that delivery arrived on a ship and saved them. More than once, the bishop saved people who were drowning in the sea, and he found miraculous ways to release people from captivity and imprisonment.

At an old age, Bishop Nicholas peacefully fell asleep in the Lord after a long life of serving others. As Patriarch Pavle would say in a sermon honoring him,

Throughout his whole life, St. Nicholas was merciful. How much he helped the poor by giving in such a way that the left hand would not know what the right one was giving! He boldly stood up for those who, not fearing for their lives, were unjustly before God condemned by the powerful ones of this world.[4]

After a lifetime of caring for his flock, watching over those in need, and being a myrrhbearer in so many senses of the word, he began to bear myrrh in a very new and literal way: His body did not decay after his death, and his incorrupt relics began to flow with myrrh. Many were healed when they were anointed with this myrrh. Even the hymns with which we honor St. Nicholas refer to myrrh. His Akathist opens,

> O champion wonderworker and superb servant of Christ, thou who pourest out for all the world the most precious myrrh of mercy and an inexhaustible sea of miracles, I praise thee with love, O Saint Nicholas; and as thou art one having boldness toward the Lord, from all dangers do thou deliver us, that we may cry to thee: Rejoice, O Nicholas, Great Wonderworker![5]

Saint Nicholas pours out "myrrh of mercy," both figuratively in the miracles he works and literally, as the myrrh that flows from his relics becomes the healing oil of Holy Unction: "Seeing the effusion of thy myrrh, O divinely wise one, our souls and bodies are enlightened, understanding thee to be a wonderful, living source of unction, O Nicholas." His role as bishop further enriches the imagery of the myrrh: "With divine myrrh the divine grace of the Spirit anointed thee, who didst preside as leader over Myra, and having made the ends of the world fragrant with the myrrh of virtues thou holiest of men."

---

4   Patriarch Pavle, 129.
5   *Akathist and Life and Miracles of Saint Nicholas the Wonderworker* (Holy Trinity Publications), 3.

The Akathist speaks of literal myrrh in the anointing of Bishop Nicholas and in the miraculous effusion of his relics, but more importantly, it recognizes the myrrh of virtues that accumulated in his heart throughout his lifetime. Like the wise virgins holding lamps filled with the oil of virtues to shine the light of Christ (Matt. 25:1–13), St. Nicholas's lamp radiates endlessly, fueled by so much oil of compassion and love that it overflows—even to the point of pouring forth from his holy relics as a healing blessing to the world.

FOR REFLECTION

- Why was it important to St. Nicholas that he do his myrrh-bearing in secret?

- Have you ever been the recipient of secret assistance? Have you ever been helped openly, in public view? How do these experiences differ?

- Christ enjoins us, "When you do a charitable deed, do not let your left hand know what your right hand is doing, that your charitable deed may be in secret" (Matt. 6:3–4). Much of St. Nicholas's giving was done in secret, but at the same time, he is one of best known and most famous saints of all time. How is it possible to be conspicuously good while keeping our Lord's commandments? How did the myrrhbearing saints we have discussed maintain their humility and love of God while also becoming known for their works?

HERMAN OF ALASKA

As Orthodox people in America, we are accustomed to seeing the Faith brought to us by immigrants who build Orthodox churches that remind them of home, and who gather together to worship in their old language among their countrymen. These immigrant churches tend to be a refuge for people weary from life in an unfamiliar land, but they are not necessarily missionary in nature.

What many Americans do not know is that the Orthodox Church sent a missionary presence to America in the eighteenth century. In 1793, just ten years after Russia acquired the Alaska Territory, the Russian Church sent a group of monks there from Valaam Monastery, in the hopes of evangelizing the native Alaskan population. They intended to translate services and Scriptures into the local languages and to establish Orthodoxy among the people of Alaska. Indeed, Russia even tried to send a bishop to Alaska with the express hope of ordaining native priests so that the indigenous population would grow into its own Aleutian Orthodoxy. It is hard to say what might have happened if this bishop's life had not ended in tragedy before reaching our continent.

Missionary Work

The first American to be canonized as an Orthodox saint was St. Herman, who was one of nine monks who journeyed from Valaam Monastery when Russia began sending fur traders to Alaska.[1] Their voyage was difficult and took nearly a full year, but when they arrived in Alaska, they received a warm reception. In every port and village they entered, people flocked to them. By the time they arrived on Kodiak Island, where they would make their home, they had baptized thousands of eager indigenous people. The main difficulty was that the native people had a tradition of what the monks called *polygamy*. By this they meant what is often called "serial monogamy": The Kodiak natives were dissolving marriages and choosing new spouses with great frequency. The monks tried, with mixed luck, to teach them that this was not acceptable for Christians. Many were baptized then went back to their villages and lived much as they had before.

Some of the monks traveled through Alaska to preach the gospel, and others settled, at least for the first few years, in Pavloskia ("St. Paul") Harbor on Kodiak Island, where the fur company had set up a small town. Father Herman was among those who remained in town, and he commented in a letter to his spiritual father at Valaam:

> With all my sorrows, I find nothing so cheers me as when I hear discussions among the brothers about preaching and about dividing various regions among themselves for that purpose, . . . a consolation and a joy for a wretch like me.[2]

---

1   Biographical information is from *Herman, A Wilderness Saint: From Savor, Russia to Kodiak, Alaska,* and the account published at https://www.oca.org/saints/lives, August 9, "Glorification of Venerable Herman of Alaska, Wonderworker of All America."

2   Sergei Korsun and Lydia Black, *Herman, A Wilderness Saint: From Sarov,*

While Fr. Herman was not called to travel into the far reaches of the Alaskan territory, to preach to the native tribes, he was overjoyed and felt unworthy even to be adjacent to such an effort. His heart was clearly devoted to the mission of bringing Christ to the indigenous people of Alaska.

Exploitation and Struggle

Upon their arrival, the monks settled into the small town built by the fur company, which had come to Alaska solely to exploit its natural resources and its people. In these early years of the Russian presence they did so mercilessly. The company's labor force was mostly indigenous. Working conditions were poor, and death rates were high. The Russians forcibly took native women as concubines; they drank heavily, caroused, and generally behaved abominably. In his diary, written ten years after their arrival, Hieromonk Gideon described watching the company's representatives force native men to go on dangerous missions shackled and at gunpoint. He then described the situation for the families they left behind:

> A compassionate person can hardly hold back tears while seeing these unfortunate people in such a condition, that they more closely resemble corpses than living beings. After the departure of the men on an expedition, those left in the settlements are women with young children and the withered old men and women. Due to the lack of *baidarkas* (boats) as well as the quit-rents imposed on them by the company involving cleaning fish, digging daylilies, and gathering berries in the summer, they do not have the

Russia to Kodiak, Alaska, trans. Fr. Daniel Marshall (Holy Trinity Publications, 2012), 33–4.

time to put up stores for themselves of the necessary food for the winter and therefore it often happens that many die of hunger.[3]

The monks had great sorrow and compassion for the way the people were treated, but they had no real recourse or authority beyond sending letters back to Russia—which they did, describing the terrible situation they'd discovered. Ultimately, they too were at the mercy of the fur company.

It is not surprising that the company, with its immoral, exploitative behavior, would be hostile to the spiritual mission of the monks. They had no interest in church for themselves and certainly did not want anyone encouraging or assisting the indigenous people. Early on in the mission, one of the monks, Fr. Macarius, was nearly killed for speaking out against the terrible treatment of the local people. He left for Russia in 1796 to inform the authorities there about what was happening in Alaska.

The company barely tolerated the presence of the monks and did nothing to help them. The monks were offered beds in a barrack where visitors came to visit concubines—literally in the same room where the monks would sleep. This of course was unacceptable, so instead the monks all lodged in a small nearby building without proper chinking. The cold Alaskan winter air entered freely. Though the Church sent money to support the mission, the company stole it and never provided the monks with food, firewood, candles, or other provisions. The monks were placed in charge of a school that had only five students because most of the children were expected to work. The company provided no supplies for the school—neither textbooks nor Bibles, paper, or slates.

---

3   Korsun, 42.

Back in Russia, Fr. Macarius made his report, and the Church determined that they must send reinforcements. The indigenous population had so embraced Christianity that Church officials decided to send a bishop to Alaska so that he could ordain local priests who would serve their own people. To this end, they established a new diocese, and in 1799, Joseph, the new bishop of Kodiak, set sail for America. With him he brought several married priests and other clergy, along with Fr. Macarius, to reinforce the Church in Alaska so that it might flourish.

The ship sank on its journey, and there were no survivors. And between 1798 and 1802, not a single ship successfully made it from Kodiak back to Russia; no letters were delivered, and no communication existed. The monks on Kodiak Island effectively were cut off from the outside world, and things went from bad to worse.

The indigenous people would come to the monks, very upset about how they were being treated. The sympathetic monks tried to help, but anything they did excited the anger of the company leadership. By 1800, the fur traders simply forbade the monks to speak to the Americans (the indigenous people of Kodiak) at all. Any encounters between the monks and the company resulted in threats of imprisonment and violence, and finally the monks were placed under house arrest. For more than a year they could not leave their little building at all, and they were guarded by armed gunmen. They did not even go to the church they had built but celebrated their services at home.

In September of 1802, ships finally began to make the journey between Russia and Alaska again, and the pressure eased on the monks. They were able to worship in their church, and they successfully notified the Church at home about the situation in Alaska. The leadership in Russia had assumed that the Kodiak mission was doing well, with a newly installed bishop and a healthy supply of clergy. They were shocked to find that the bishop they sent had never arrived and that the monks on Kodiak Island, along with the indigenous people, were suffering so badly. Only four members of the original mission were still alive. The Russian government began to send leaders to oversee activities in Alaska. The Church sent Fr. Gideon to restore order in Kodiak, and for the most part, he was successful. He was able to pressure the fur company into better behavior.

Spruce Island

By 1807, living conditions were improving. Herman even was able to befriend the company leadership and to provide some influence over their treatment of the indigenous people. Herman loved everyone and considered every person a friend, whether they returned his sentiments or not. In a letter back to Russia he wrote, "I get along with everyone though some curse me."[4] The indigenous people helped the monks to farm, and they shared their harvest generously. He was incredibly popular in the little town, and when he went out for a walk, children would flock to him to hear another story of a saint's life. He enjoyed the people there in town, but he truly missed the quiet, contemplative life of a hermit.

At some point between 1811 and 1817, the monks began to split off to create sketes in the wilderness. Herman chose Spruce Island as his new home. The small, forested island, a two-hour boat ride from the harbor and the church in town, reminded him of Valaam. With his own hands, he built himself a little cell with a garden in front, and the community added a wooden school for orphans and a guesthouse nearby. He also built a small chapel where he would invite the Aleut families and orphans to worship on Sundays. He

---

4   Korsun, 87.

taught at the school and enjoyed the children very much. He would make big platters of pretzels and *krendelki* (cookies) for them, and they adored him. He wrote home to Valaam:

> I live about almost seven miles from the Harbor on a separate small island, the name of which is New Valaam. Nearby me there is a very small brook; there is enough fish in it in the summer. I live alone. Only about 1.3 miles away there is a family of three Americans; when I am in need, they help me with great love.
>
> Father Joseph often visits me on the small American leather boats, which are locally called *baidarkas*. We have gardens together and share everything. The Americans who live near me consider us natives and help us in everything.[5]

Herman loved the Americans, and they loved him as well. He lived an ascetic life filled with labor. He raised potatoes and cabbage and other vegetables, handling all the work himself, carrying a heavy basket of seaweed from the shore to his garden to fertilize the soil. It happened that one night, his disciple, Gerasim, saw him walking barefoot in the cold Alaskan winter, carrying a large log which weighed enough to require four men to lift. Father Herman humbly hid his ascetic labors, but others glimpsed them here and there. He would wear 13.5-pound chains to weigh himself down, and he slept on a hard board with bricks for pillows and another hard board for a blanket. He ate very little. He spent much time in his cell praying, and the people outside could hear him chanting and singing the services, according to the monastic rule. Everything he acquired through these labors—both his spiritual gifts and the fruits of the earth—was used for the feeding and clothing of the orphans and books for the school.

---

5   Korsun, 120.

Years of Loving Ministry

Herman was not shy to complain when people were mistreated by the company, or to intercede before the governors on behalf of one who had transgressed. He defended those who had been offended and helped those in need. The Alutiiq, known to the Russians as Aleuts, liked to visit him to ask advice and help with various difficulties they were facing. He sat patiently and listened to every single one, and he did everything in his power to help. He was often called upon to settle disputes, and he was an excellent mediator, especially at reestablishing peace in families. In those situations where a husband and wife could not be reconciled, Herman asked them to separate, even if only temporarily, for he said,

> It is better to let them live apart, so that they not fight and quarrel, or believe me—it is scary; if they are not separated, there have been instances that the husband killed the wife, or that the wife tormented the husband.[6]

He ministered to the people based on the reality of their situation and in the interest of protecting and helping them. He was not concerned with lecturing them on proper moral behavior but met them where they were and helped to guide them to better and better ways.

At one point, a ship from the United States brought a terrible influenza to Sitka and Kodiak Island that was killing people in the course of about three days. Kodiak Island had no doctors and no medicine, and the flu spread rapidly. Entire families died. The death toll was so high that there were not enough people to dig graves, and the bodies piled up. This horrific epidemic continued

---

6   Korsun, 126–7.

for a month, and Herman alone tirelessly visited the sick. Though his own life was certainly in danger, he counseled as many dying people as he could, comforting them and preparing them for death. As a result, the people who survived this epidemic loved him even more.

In addition to loving people, Herman also loved animals. He always kept dried fish for the birds, and they would gather in great numbers around his cell. Underneath his cell, an ermine made her den. Even when she had babies, and would ordinarily fight anyone who dared approach, Herman would feed her from his own hand. But most amazingly, it happened frequently that people would come upon Herman as he was feeding bears. The area around his little cell was surrounded by his beautiful garden and many wild creatures, all of whom came gently to him.

At one point a terrible flood occurred, and the people on Spruce Island came to him, terrified. He placed an icon of the Theotokos from the school building on a sandy bank and began to pray. Then he turned to the group and said calmly, "Have no fear, the water will not go any higher than the place where this holy icon stands." And indeed, it did not.

Herman arrived in Alaska a quiet and kind monk, but by the end of his long life, God had turned him into a wonderworker. Over the years, he braved various kinds of danger, from nature and from other people, but his faith was steadfast throughout, and he was happy to endure any struggle as a love offering to God. He took on ascetic labors, served others with great joy and devotion, and put his fate entirely in God's hands—all as an offering to God, who would receive his offering and multiply it. He is defined and marked by his genuine love for others: for God, for his countrymen, and especially for the Americans, the indigenous people of Alaska.

FOR REFLECTION

• The monks arrived on Kodiak Island to find that the fur trading company was shockingly exploitative and immoral. Have you ever encountered a situation where people were being mistreated? What can be done about it?

• Though he patiently spent years on Kodiak Island, St. Herman yearned for the solitude of a cell in the woods and moved to Spruce Island as soon as he was able. Many monastics live away from the city, in the desert or forest, and even Jesus Himself frequently withdrew to the wilderness to pray (Luke 5:16). Where do you find solitude and peace?

• What do you think is the benefit of sleeping between boards, with bricks for pillows?

OLGA OF ALASKA

I n the years since St. Herman and his contemporaries built missions in Alaska, Orthodoxy has continued to grow among the native population as well as claiming converts from other backgrounds along the way. There are now around ninety active Orthodox parishes in Alaska, and the state has produced several saints. The most recent of them to be canonized—on June 19, 2025— is St. Olga, known locally as St. Olga of Kwethluk. She lived a quiet life of service—and yet, hers was an ordinary life, not unlike someone you might know.

Because she was the wife of a priest, she was known as Matushka Olga. *Matushka* is a Russian word that means "mother," and in her case this maternal title really fits. According to her daughter, Anita,

> Mom was approachable. I mean, she was like the mom of the whole village. . . . Even people from the villages, they would stop by and instead of saying, "How's Arrsamaq?" they'd say, "How's Mom?" Like she's everybody's mom. I mean, that's how you felt around her. She was a mom, and she was willing to take care of you.[1]

---

1 *The Life of My Grandmother*, https://scholarworks.alaska.edu/handle /11122/12645, 65. This beautiful article is offered by St. Olga's granddaughter, O. J. Skinner, who interviewed people close to the saint to

Olga was a myrrhbearing saint if ever there was one: People could sense that she was available to them. Another of her daughters said,

> She had lots of friends. The whole village was her friends, and all the people were friends. If she took a walk up the village she would have ten or twelve kids with her. Some of them are my cousins, and some of them are somebody's kids. Lots of kids used to be with her. They seem to like to be with her. I don't know why. But her house was always full. She never seem to push away any people. Even when they're drunk or acting crazy she never push them away. She just talked to them even though they don't want to talk, but they want to be with her.[2]

People felt Olga's acceptance, and she drew them into her home, offering hospitality and love without judgment.

Tomboy

In 1916, Olga was born into an indigenous Alaskan Yup'ik family. She was named Arrsamquq and as an infant was baptized Olga, and people called her Olinka. Even as a young child, her life was imbued with the love of God. She was the eldest of all the children in the family, and the only girl—so as you might expect, she played with boys and became quite a tomboy.

Like many of the native people in her area, Olga's family lived in town only a short part of the year for Christmas (on the old

---

produce a wonderful portrait of Olga as a human being in context—in her culture, among her people. This paper is a treasure and gives wonderful insights into Olga's culture, personality, and habits. All quotations are reproduced directly from the transcript.

2   *The Life of My Grandmother*, 95.

calendar, January 7) and stayed for a while thereafter. But they spent most of the year in the mountains, herding reindeer. Her granddaughter recalls,

> Life in the mountains certainly made an impression on my grandmother. My mother, Anita, remembered she loved the mountains. There's a couple times Dad took us all the way up to the mountains, and I remember that one time, she missed being up there. When we got up there she said, "If anything happens to me, you can bury me right here."[3]

Olga spent the majority of her young life in the mountains, and she told her children and grandchildren stories of those times. The stories were often funny and charming. For example, as her granddaughter explains,

> My grandmother and her friend were walking together when they came upon a particular reindeer that was known to be mean. When it saw them, it began running after them. Her friend was able to grab a large rock before they ended up climbing up a tree. When the reindeer was below them, the friend dropped the rock. The reindeer fell over dead. The two climbed down the tree. . . . When they came down, they said, "Oh, look what we did. What are we going to tell so and so [the reindeer's owner]?" In those days, when you did something wrong you tell that person what you did. So they were walking there and just when they met that person, they were trying to tell in a gentler way, "Oh, we killed your reindeer." Olinka happened to look over his shoulder. There was the reindeer, staggering towards them. Olinka was so relieved.[4]

---

3   *Life of My Grandmother*, 26.
4   *Life of My Grandmother*, 29–30.

Up in the mountains, in addition to herding reindeer, the families hunted, fished, and trapped animals. Olga had a particular strategy: She put *meluk* (fish eggs) on her fingers like rings to bait the fish, and then she dropped her hand into the water and waited patiently. When a fish came by to nibble the eggs, she would grab it and pull it out of the water.

When they were in town at the beginning of each year, the family attended church. Olga knew many liturgical texts and hymns by heart, in both Church Slavonic and Yup'ik, including those from Holy Week and Pascha. Life in this remote Alaska town was hard, and villagers lost a lot of people in various outbreaks of illnesses like tuberculosis and smallpox. With so much death, poverty, and struggle around them, Olga held fast to the Church and to Christ.

Married Life

Shortly before her nineteenth birthday, Olga married Nicolai O. Michael. The marriage had been arranged for them, and from that day forward, her life changed dramatically. For one thing, she no longer lived in the mountains for much of the year, though Nicolai was adept at both fishing and hunting. Instead, he worked in town year-round, establishing a general store and opening the first post office in their village. In those early years, the newly married couple struggled; their marriage was filled with strife and arguments. Nicolai was not interested in church, and his friends weren't believers.

Olga prayed intensely for her husband and all his friends, asking God to act on his heart. Through her prayers, he began to attend church and brought six of his friends with him. Soon, they all were tonsured as readers. Nicolai went on to study at "Aleut School," a small local school run by the Church, much like those set up by St.

Innocent during his years in Alaska. When he graduated, he was ordained to the priesthood. From 1963 on, he served his village of Kwethluk and was greatly beloved by his people.

When Nicolai became a priest, their lives changed again. Father Nicolai traveled extensively to twelve surrounding villages to conduct services. He didn't travel on roads, but on rivers—in a boat in warmer weather and on a dogsled or snowmobile in cold weather. Matushka Olga, who was the only able midwife in the region, accompanied her husband on his trips so she could be available to assist women in childbirth and anyone else who was sick or struggling. As the matushka, she now was connected in a new way to the people of the surrounding villages, and she quietly gave them food and clothing, sewing little baby booties for them, and midwifed them through childbirth and, in some cases, child loss.

Father Nicolai and Olga had thirteen children, and Olga delivered only one of them in a hospital. The other twelve children were born at home. Sometimes Olga's mother was present to assist her, but many times, Olga gave birth alone. She must have understood very well the value for the women of Alaska of having a midwife taking care of them.

Three of Olga's children died as infants, and two died around the age of three years old. One of the three-year-olds, Timothy, died along with many others when an epidemic raged up and down the Kuskokwim River. Families in the villages absorbed not just their own children's deaths, but the losses of their friends and neighbors; everyone mourned. I would imagine that in the local school, there were classes whose numbers were unnaturally small because of deaths from epidemics. Olga and her community lost many children in this way over the years, and yet, these traumatic deaths were also the normal course of things, a predictable and recurring misery.

When we suffer great loss, we have a choice: We can turn on God, blaming Him and isolating ourselves, or we can turn *to* God, knowing that He weeps with us, and invite Him to carry us through dark times. Olga must have leaned on God even more as she experienced this suffering, burying her own children as she had buried so many neighbors over the years. Through all of it, she remained open, loving, and welcoming. She even took in a grand-daughter, Elizabeth, who came into her home at age three and lived with Olga until high school.

Hospitality

Olga liked to take people into her home. As Martha recalls,

> We were living in one house—Mom, Dad, me, my great grandma, my Auntie Martha (Aiyanguq), and an orphaned old woman. In those days, when people did not have anybody to take care of them, they were taken in and cared for without letting them go hungry or want for things. That dear old woman, Nay-agaurluq, had the name Ephenia. We took care of her. I liked sleeping beside her.[5]

It seems to have been a cultural expectation that those who could not provide for themselves would be "adopted" into homes, and accordingly, Olga and her family were happy to take in an orphaned (that is, widowed) woman in need.

Olga took care of many others as well. As Anita explained,

> She would cook us sourdough pancakes . . . then she'd always do something like pack water, or chop wood, then she'd check on

---

5   *Life of My Grandmother*, 33.

Grandma and see how she's doing or whoever she knew needed help, she'd check on them too.[6]

Olga worked cheerfully without much rest, simply doing what was needed and what might make life better for the people around her. Not only did she help others with their housekeeping, but she also made boots, parkas, socks, and mittens to distribute among the parishioners. For her acts of charity, she was nicknamed "the new righteous Tabitha," after the beloved maker of coats and garments for the poor (Acts 9:39).

She taught her children by example and by putting them to work as well, scrubbing clothes and diapers. They "did laundry, packed water, and dumped honey buckets[7] for widowers and others." Father Nicolai also built a house for an orphaned old woman, and their oldest daughter, Martha, move in with her to helped take care of her.[8]

Following their mother's lead—and command—the sisters learned how to serve others and carried on Olga's tradition of myrrhbearing long into the future. As her daughter Lillian wrote,

From her, we learned to love and have compassion for children. When I was growing up we'd have a whole bunch of kids in here whose parents, in one way or another, didn't take care of them. . . . We always had lots of kids in here and that's how I think the love for children that she had within her was given to us. And the children that we used to take care of are now adults and they do talk about those times when they would have to come here just so they could have a roof over their heads, warm

---

6 *Life of My Grandmother*, 36.
7 A toilet made of a plastic container with a seat on top.
8 *Life of My Grandmother*, 37–8.

place and some place where there's food. I think we inherited that from her because our love for the children is reflected in our jobs.[9]

Olga's children became teachers and social workers—myrrhbearers, carrying on their myrrhbearing mother's tradition.

Olga was especially mindful of the troubled women who suffered from domestic violence. She would invite women into the privacy of a traditional Yup'ik steam bath—a wooden structure with a hot stone in the center, surrounded by benches—where women would sit naked, their bruises and cuts exposed. This space, both intimate and honest, allowed Olga to offer kindness and healing to the women, helping to lift any burden of grief or shame. Many people observed that Olga spoke with a deep understanding of the experience of physical and sexual abuse, leading them to believe that she too had suffered such violence in her life.

After the Funeral

In 1979, at age 63, Matushka Olga's beautiful life of service was ended by cancer. On her last day, she received Holy Communion, crossed herself, and departed peacefully to God. Since her death, people all over the world have experienced visits from Matushka Olga, often related to the trauma of sexual abuse. The best-known account comes from New York, a great distance from her home in Alaska, where a woman was healed in an encounter with Olga and wrote to Olga's family to tell them about it.[10]

One day, the woman was praying and began to have an intense flashback of her sexual abuse as a child. She pleaded with the

---

9   *Life of My Grandmother*, 48.
10   Evan Erickson, "St. Olga of Kwethluk to become first-ever Yup'ik saint," *Alaska Public Media*, December 15, 2023, https://alaskapublic .org/2023/12/15/st-olga-of-kwethluk-to-become-first-ever-yupik-saint/.

Mother of God for help, and slowly, she went into a sort of trance and saw herself walking in a forest. A gentle wave of tenderness began to sweep through the woods, followed by a fresh garden scent. She saw the Virgin Mary walking toward her. As she approached, the woman became aware that Mary was not alone; an indigenous woman followed her. The Mother of God identified her as St. Olga.

Saint Olga gestured for the woman to follow her to a little hill with a door cut into the side. Olga helped her up on a bed and rubbed something on her belly. The woman's belly looked five months pregnant, although she was not actually pregnant. Mother Olga pretended to labor with her. The woman pushed out something like an afterbirth, and she was filled with wellness. A sense of quiet entered her soul. As the woman recalled, St. Olga's eyes spoke with great tenderness and understanding. It was the kind of loving gaze from a mother to an infant that connects and welcomes a baby to life. After some time, St. Olga told her, "The people who hurt you thought they could make you carry their evil inside of you by rape. That's a lie. The only thing they could put inside you was the seed of life, which is a creation of God and cannot pollute anyone."

At the end of this healing time, the two walked outside together. The sky was shimmering with a moving veil of light. The woman heard in her heart that this curtain of light was a promise that God can create great beauty from complete desolation and nothingness.

In honor of this vision, St. Olga's icons show her holding a scroll with the same words: "God can create great beauty from complete desolation," for her lifetime was spent working in synergy with God, caring for grieving, struggling, and suffering people. Olga had a gift for understanding women especially, for seeing their trauma and pain, and for helping them release it and be healed. In this sense, she served as a spiritual guide in addition to all the practical care, from medical care and midwifery to food and clothing and shoes, that she so generously bestowed on the neighbors God sent her. Matushka Olga's world was filled with pain and struggle, but she both found and created beauty within it. She knew Christ's light and worked to shine it on every person she met.

Saint Olga's story is especially wonderful because of its simplicity. She was not a monastic, not a great ascetic, neither an apostle nor a missionary. She was a normal woman, living in community with other normal women. She shared their struggles and joys because she was one of them. How appropriate and beautiful that the first American woman to be canonized was so focused on women's issues: pregnancy, miscarriage, childbirth, infant and child loss, rape and sexual trauma. She had a husband and children and was not unlike someone you may know at church: one of many very faithful and productive women who dedicate all their energy to service.

Over the centuries, many men and women have worked out their salvation in much the same way as St. Olga, through quiet service to their families while also making the whole world their family. Not many of these people will be recognized as saints, but perhaps more of them should be. Thank God, Olga is known to us, a motherly myrrhbearer who is always ready to help.

FOR REFLECTION

- Saint Olga and her community experienced many tragic losses due to epidemics and illnesses. How do you suppose such losses impact a community? Can loss create any kind of opportunity for beauty?

- Saint Olga was a mother to everyone who knew her. How can we go about becoming mothers and fathers to people outside our families?

- Saint Olga is especially beloved for her work with women who suffered abuse, and yet little is known of those stories. What does it mean to have a saint who understands and addresses the deep pains we don't talk about?

BISHOP BASIL RODZIANKO

The Orthodox know countless holy martyrs from the Communist years in Russia; the prison camps, or gulags, were famously harsh, with intense forced labor, starvation, inhumanly cold temperatures, and general cruelty and torture. Against this stark and terrible backdrop, we see the lives of many saints lived out, but we also see that many well-educated Russians were exiled or escaped then found each other in communities around Western Europe, planting the seeds of Orthodoxy in unexpected places. One of them, Bishop Basil Rodzianko, liked to say, "The Providence of God brings good out of evil."[1] His story is living proof.

When the Russian Revolution began in 1917, Vladimir Rodzianko was just two years old. His mother was a Russian baroness, and his father's father served multiple terms as the president of the Russian Imperial Duma.[2] The Rodzianko family, aristocratic and influential in the Tsarist regime, was now on the revolutionaries' death list. They fled to Belgrade, where Vladimir would eventually meet a man who also was living in exile and would become his spiritual father: St. John Maximovitch.

---

1 Elissa Davis Bjeletich, host, *Everyday Orthodox* podcast, "Bishop Basil Rodzianko," Ancient Faith Ministries, April 20, 2018, https://www.ancientfaith.com/podcasts/everydayorthodox/bishop_basil_rodzianko/.

2 The Russian Imperial Duma was the lower house of Russia's parliament from 1906 to 1917.

Vladimir grew up in Belgrade and married Vasilyena, who was also the child of Russian exiles. Shortly after, he was ordained to the priesthood. When World War II broke out, Fr. Vladimir did everything he could to help suffering people. He was part of the Serbian resistance, rescuing Serbs from concentration camps, and he and his wife adopted an orphaned Ukrainian girl. When the Communist dictator Tito came to power, Fr. Vladimir still was serving as a priest in Serbia. At that point, most of the Russian émigrés had left the country, but Fr. Vladimir stayed to serve his parish. In July 1949 he was arrested and sentenced to eight years in the gulag for producing illegal religious propaganda. After years of hard labor, the prison officials realized he could be put to better use. According to his secretary and friend, Marilyn Swezey,

> He was assigned to listen to Western broadcasts and translate them because of his knowledge of languages. And . . . in listening to all this, he realized what an effect broadcasting could have on imprisoned people.[3]

His time in the gulag was terrible, and yet God brought something good out of it, for there Fr. Vladimir was inspired to become a broadcaster, encouraging those in captivity with the gospel message.

The Power of Radio

When Fr. Vladimir was released from prison, he and his wife went to Paris until Bishop Nikolai Velimirovich invited him to come serve at the Cathedral of St. Sava of Serbia in London. Father Vladimir agreed and immediately pursued an additional career: He got a job at the British Broadcasting Corporation. Father knew that

---

3   *Everyday Orthodox.*

he wanted to create a Russian-language religious program to broadcast into Russia, but it took him a while to convince the BBC. Of course, he had the courage of his convictions and was an intelligent and persuasive man. His persistence was rewarded, and the station let him use the studios late at night when the BBC was off the air.

Father recorded long talks on the Faith as well as all his sermons, and sometimes he recorded services at the Russian cathedral in London, broadcasting everything in the Russian language. The radio waves penetrated the Iron Curtain, carrying the gospel and the riches of the Orthodox Faith into the Soviet Union. The BBC started getting letters from the far corners of Russia, thanking them for these broadcasts. The executives were amazed at the power of these religious broadcasts and at the impact one priest recording sermons late at night could have on the world.

Father Vladimir was often the only Orthodox priest that many people in the Soviet Union were able to hear. His radio ministry was tremendous, and "through this program many, many generations of citizens of the USSR learned something about God, about their holy Orthodox Faith, and also about the history of their Church and their country."[4] Marilyn said that in later years, when he traveled to Russia,

> He would meet hierarchs and seminarians alike who would say, "Oh, we've been listening to you." They would find a way to go outside the cities where they could get the shortwave radio broadcasts, avoiding the jamming from the Soviet technology, of course. He started these broadcasts in 1955, and they continued until his death in 1999.[5]

---

4   Archimandrite Tikhon Shevkunov and Julian Henry Lowenfeld, *Everyday Saints and Other Stories*, (repr. in English, Pokrov Publications, 2013), 74.
5   *Everyday Orthodox.*

Inspired by his experiences in the gulag, Fr. Vladimir found a way to nourish Orthodoxy under communism, even across great distances. He became a faraway but intimate spiritual father to thousands.

Obedience

Father adored his wife, Matushka Maria, and when she passed away, he was devastated. He continued to serve as a priest and to do his radio shows, but he was miserable. During this difficult period he began drinking heavily, and as he described it, became an alcoholic. One night, his beloved wife came to him in a dream and told him to straighten up. He was so struck by her visit and her message that he stopped drinking immediately. But his grief remained. His children were grown, and he was alone. What was he to do with himself? He prayed for guidance.

He didn't have to wait long for an answer. After St. John Maximovitch fell asleep in the Lord in 1966, Fr. Vladimir's new spiritual father was Metropolitan Anthony Bloom. The metropolitan came to him with interesting news: The Orthodox Church in America was hoping he would take monastic vows and become their bishop in Washington, DC. At age 66, he became a monk and received the new name, Basil. Of course, many bishops serve in obedience as monks for decades before ever being elevated to any kind of authority, but he was on a fast track: He would take his vows and be elevated immediately.

This plan worried Father, so he approached the metropolitan with his concerns:

"Well, I mean," Father Vladimir reasoned, "instead of just starting me out as a simple monk, you're immediately making me a bishop. In other words, instead of being a novice and obeying the commands of others, my job will mean that I'm the one who will have to command and make decisions. How then do I fulfill the vow of obedience? . . . Whom will I obey?"

Metropolitan Anthony grew thoughtful for a moment, and then said: "You will be in obedience to everyone and anyone whom you meet on your journey through life. As long as that person's request will be within your power to grant it, and not in contradiction with the Scriptures."[6]

Father Vladimir loved this idea, and so he became Bishop Basil, the hierarch who answered to his people. Whenever someone interrupted his day with a request, he always agreed to answer it with great joy and sincerity. In doing so, he found an obedience that would allow him to die to himself, training him to submit his will to God and to love his neighbor with all his heart and soul.

In his later years, after *perestroika*, Bishop Basil was able to visit Russia several times. Archimandrite (now Metropolitan of Pskov and Porkhov) Tikhon was with him on those visits and tells the story of a little old lady who called out to the bishop on the streets of Moscow, "Father! Can't you help me? Please, come and bless my room!" People who did not even know him, but who recognized the cassock, would often produce a request out of the blue, and he would agree, joyful in his obedience. So he canceled his plans and followed a stranger all the way across the city to bless her room. The old woman was so happy to be with Bishop Basil, telling him all about her grandchildren who could never visit, and her loneliness faded as she reveled in the company and attention of a kindly man of God. He blessed her room:

6   Shevkunov, 383.

with sincerest prayer, majestically, and triumphantly, just the way he always performed any divine services. Then he sat down with the ecstatic Grandma (actually, both of them were ecstatic about each other) and praised to the skies her humble offerings—little Russian pretzels called sushki, and tea. . . . Then, with immense gratitude, he accepted as an honor and did not refuse the crumpled one ruble note that she stealthily handed to her "Father" as she said goodbye. "May the Lord save you!" she called out to the bishop! "Now it will be sweet for me to die in this little room!"[7]

This woman was hungry for company and conversation, and the bishop fed her with love and affection. Ironically, he was able to feed her by accepting food from her hand, but that is no less a myrrhbearing act. Bishop Basil was a true servant, happy to obey his sheep and delighted to spend time with those whom God's Providence put on his path.

Ultimately, it wasn't exactly the people he was obeying. Bishop Basil was obeying God. As Archimandrite Tikhon observed,

Gradually I begin to grasp that it was through this humble vow of service and obedience, remaining a novice even upon attaining the rank of a very senior cleric, that our sovereign Bishop Basil taught himself how to sensitively hear and to obey the will of God. Because of this, his entire life was nothing more and not less than one constant search for the knowledge of the will of God, one mysterious yet absolutely real conversation with our Savior, in which He would speak to mankind not with words, but with the circumstances of this life, while granting unto His

---

7   Shevkunov, 384–5.

listeners the very greatest reward there is—a chance to be His instrument in this world.[8]

In Conversation with Christ

By always saying yes, Bishop Basil entered into a mystical conversation with Christ. Our Savior spoke with circumstances instead of words—and Bishop Basil answered Him in kind by serving everyone with a joyful and loving heart. Could this be the language of God? Does God speak myrrhbearer?

If he ever wondered if God's Providence guided him through his unusual obedience, according to Marilyn, one event "really deeply impressed Bishop Basil." He had set aside some very important plans because a young priest asked him to come to his church, which was in a small town, many hours off the path the bishop had planned to travel. They had been driving for hours, headed into the middle of nowhere, when they happened upon the scene of a car accident. A father was dead, and his son sat by the roadside in grief and shock.

The bishop got out of the car and embraced the young man, offering to pray a memorial service if the man was Christian and would want one. The son confirmed that he was a Christian but clarified that because there were no parishes in the area, his father didn't really go to church; he was an Orthodox Christian and had a spiritual father, but the son didn't know him. The bishop was curious and asked, "How is it that he came to have a spiritual father but did not go to church?" He then listened in amazement as the son answered that his father called this man his spiritual father, but really he was a priest named Rodzianko broadcasting from

---

8   Shevkunov, 385–6.

across the world. The bishop stared at the young man and told him that he was the priest Rodzianko. Overcome, the bishop "sobbed and wept and got down on his knees before his spiritual son who had just died."[9] He prayed the *panikhida* and helped the man's son arrange an Orthodox funeral, honoring his spiritual son with all the love and care of the myrrhbearing bishop he had become.

Bishop Basil's example of saying yes, of setting aside his own plans in order to serve his neighbor, is within reach of all of us. We too can enter into conversation with Christ; we can learn to listen for the way He speaks through circumstance and Providence and master the language of myrrhbearing. Like the good Samaritan, who was going somewhere else when a beaten man appeared along his path, we can try to remember that our plans are not more important than whomever God sends our way. We can stop worshiping the idol of our own agendas and learn to make an offering at the altar of the icon of Christ before us. We may not be able to say yes every time—and, truth be told, neither could the bishop—but we may well find it very worthwhile on those occasions when we do.

When Bishop Basil passed away, Marilyn says that "his first panakhida service was like Pascha. All of us there felt that. It was just Pascha. It was already in the other world." It's like that when saints pass into the next life—when we pray for their eternal memory, they seem to be praying back to us, sending us grace. Marilyn is hopeful that she'll see Bishop Basil canonized in her lifetime and says that if she writes a hagiography about him, she'll want to focus on "the theme that was in many of his sermons, in his talks, in his thinking, and especially in his life. And he often would say this: 'The Providence of God brings good out of evil.' And that really was the story of his life."[10]

---

9   Shevkunov, 387.
10 *Everyday Orthodox.*

FOR REFLECTION

• When God speaks to you, does He use words or other people and circumstances?

• Would you consider engaging in radical obedience like the bishop? Could you vow to say yes to all reasonable requests, putting your ability to plan in jeopardy?

• Why did his obedience bring him such joy?

PORPHYRIOS OF KAVSOKALYVIA

In 1906, Evangelos was born in the village of Aghios Ioannis to a devout but very poor family.[1] His father went to America to work on the Panama Canal, and all the children—from very young ages—worked to keep the farm going. Angelos often took the flocks up the mountain to graze. Though he completed only one year of school, he carried a little book about St. John the Hutdweller and read it one syllable at a time in the mountains. He had never seen a monk or visited a monastery, but he yearned to live like St. John.

The Joy of Obedience

When he was just seven years old, his mother sent him to another island to live and work in a relative's general mercantile store. The owner and his family were very kind, and they were impressed with little Evangelos's work ethic. One day, two men came into the store, and the boy overheard their conversation about Mount Athos. He was fascinated, and from that day forward thought of

---

1   Biographical information comes from *Wounded by Love* and the account at www.oca.org/saints/lives, December 2, "Saint Porphyrios, Wonderworker of Kavsokaliva."

nothing else. After multiple attempts, he finally managed to stow away on a boat and to make his way to the Holy Mountain.

Along the journey, Evangelos met a monk who invited him to join him and another elder at the hermitage of Saint George of Kavsokalyvia. As it turns out, these monks were known for being unusually austere, and they were very strict spiritual guides. By the time he was fourteen years old, Evangelos was tonsured a monk and given a new name, Nikitas. Soon he was given the highest honor a monastic can receive, being tonsured into the Great Schema. Nikitas loved living in obedience to these two elders:

> Obedience! What can I say? I truly knew the meaning of that word! I abandoned myself to obedience with joy and love. It was this absolute obedience that saved me and it was on account of this that God gave me His charismatic gift. Yes, I repeat, I was utterly obedient to my elders—not forced obedience, but with joy and love. . . . I went here and I went there. I was devoted to them. And so my soul was winged with joy when I was with them. . . . My life was prayer, joy and obedience to my elders.[2]

Nikitas (later Porphyrios) had a transformative experience when, very early in the morning before the Divine Liturgy, he snuck into the church to have some time there on his own before everyone else arrived. Another monk, Old Dimas, was already there, praying alone before the Lord:

> The outpouring and superabundance of grace flowed over my pitiful self when I saw Old Dimas making prostrations and dissolving in tears in his prayer in the Kyriakon. With the prostrations of that man, grace overshadowed him so profusely that it

---

2   Porphyrios, 12.

radiated out even over me. It was then that the richness of grace was released over me also. Certainly, the grace existed before with the love I had for my elder. But it was then that I sensed the grace with exceptional intensity. He transmitted the grace of God to me. The grace that that saint possessed radiated into my soul also. He transmitted to me his spiritual gifts of grace.[3]

Porphyrios—at this point, still known as the monk Nikitas—would live with this special charisma, these gifts of the Holy Spirit, for the rest of his life. By his own explanation, they came to him as an unearned gift from God, both because of the great love and joy he found in obedience and because the holiness of Old Dimas was so superabundant that it flowed out, pouring over the young man and radiating into his soul. This idea that grace radiates—that we can receive God's grace and then radiate it out toward others—would continue to develop throughout his life and become a major theme in his teachings.

Young Nikitas possessed what he called "clear sight"—a kind of interior vision of what was happening in the world. In one example, he could see his elders coming to him from a distance, though a hill interrupted the line of physical sight. He told his elder, "The hill was like a pane of glass and I saw you on the other side." But this gift also meant that God revealed other things to him, including insight into a person's heart. In his own words,

The gift of clear sight, as I have told you, was something that I had never desired. Nor, when I received it, did I attempt to increase it or to cultivate it. I gave no importance to it. Neither have I ever asked, nor do I ask God to reveal something to me, because I believe it is counter to His will. But after the experience

---

3   Porphyrios, 27–8.

with Dimas I changed completely. My life became all joys and exaltation. I lived among the stars, in infinity, in heaven. I wasn't like that previously.

From the moment I experienced the grace of God all the gifts were multiplied. I became sharp-witted. I learned the Trinitarian canons, the Canon of Jesus and other canons. . . . I recited the Psalter by heart.[4]

His experience of God had always been joyful, but after his experience with Dimas, his joy was superabundant—as it would be throughout his adult life. God made him "sharp-witted" so that he now could easily memorize the hymns and psalms he yearned to have written on his heart. He loved his life on Mount Athos, and the gifts God bestowed on him only made that life more joyful and more intensely beautiful. He hoped to remain on the Holy Mountain, devoted to God and his elders, for the rest of his life.

A New Chapter

God had other plans for him, however. When he was nineteen years old, Nikitas became seriously ill, and he had to leave Mount Athos. He was crushed and always hoped to return, but his health required him to eat animal products that were not available on the Holy Mountain. The gifts God had given him had another purpose: God was not just creating a monk full of exaltation and joy, but He had transformed Nikitas into a gifted spiritual father. He now had clear sight into a person's heart when they came to confess to him. His joy, combined with this new intelligence, was a charisma that made him a great spiritual healer, able to diagnose the illness and apply just the right medicine for a cure.

---

4   Porphyrios, 30.

When he was just twenty years old, Nikitas was ordained a priest and given his new name: Fr. Porphyrios. At twenty-two he was made a confessor, and for fifteen years he heard confessions continually:

> How the monks and lay people that came for confession loved me! I heard confessions there day and night non-stop. I started early in the morning and I continued all through the day and throughout the night and the next day and the next night without interruption. I went forty-eight hours without eating. Fortunately, God took care of me and gave my sister the inspiration to bring me some milk to drink. . . . They waited all night long for their turn. When they left they would say to each other, "Now there's a priest who's a knower of hearts!"[5]

God granted Fr. Porphyrios the gift of clear sight so that he could heal; his insight into people's hearts made him a confessor who could provide the best possible spiritual care for scores of pilgrims. His ministry was truly myrrhbearing: In loving compassion, he gave himself over to serving those who traveled from afar and waited for hours for his assistance, working around the clock to provide as much healing to as many people as he could.

Look to the Light

Elder Porphyrios learned over time how best to unbind people from their sins. In his own words, he explained,

> To begin with, when I first started to hear confessions, I used to really "scald" those who came to make confession. I used to

---

5   Porphyrios, 43.

have at my side Saint Nikodemos's *Confessor's Guide*. . . . If he confessed a serious sin then I would look up the book and would see that it wrote: "Not to receive Holy Communion for eighteen years." I didn't know; I was inexperienced. And so I imposed the corresponding penance. Whatever the book said was law.[6]

Elder Porphyrios naively followed the book precisely, applying strict penances without exception. Over time, however, he saw that when these people returned to him, they had stopped praying, stopped doing any of the spiritual exercises he had given them. They simply gave up: "Well, you told me that I couldn't receive Communion for eighteen years so I thought to myself, 'Since I'm damned anyway, I might as well forget about the whole thing.'"[7] The strictness of his response was impeding their recovery. As if they had received a terminal diagnosis with no hope for a cure, they didn't bother to take their medication. Elder Porphyrios changed course:

And so I started to encourage the people to read the poetic canons written in honor of the saints, to read short prayers, to make prostrations and to read Holy Scripture. And in that way they began to pay attention to the things of our religion. Their hearts were softened and without any external prompting they desired to observe the fasts, to enter the spiritual arena and to come to know Christ. And one thing I have understood is that when someone comes to know Christ and love Him and is loved by Christ, everything thereafter proceeds well in holiness and joy and everything is easy.[8]

---

6   Porphyrios, 43–4.
7   Porphyrios, 44.
8   ibid.

By turning his spiritual children toward Christ, toward beauty and goodness and truth, he found that their sins fell away. He said, "If you make someone acutely aware of his fault, this provokes a reaction in him that makes him unable to give it up later."[9] Focusing on the severity of the sin could bind that sin to a person, causing him to identify with it. Such reactions simply magnified the negative force that already was pulling this person away from God and into sin; looking away from sin and directly at Christ was the cure and the key to unbinding the penitent.

This would become another great theme of Elder Porphyrios's teaching: Rather than fighting sin—engaging with the devil and trying to win a battle—we should instead turn our attention to Christ. Then we will find that the battle dissipates:

> There are two paths that lead to God: the hard and debilitating path with fierce assaults against evil, and the easy path of love. There are many who chose the hard path and "shed blood in order to receive Spirit" until they attained great virtue. I find the shorter and safer route is the path of love. This is the path that you, too, should follow.
>
> That is, you can make a different kind of effort: to study and pray and have your aim to advance in the love of God and of the Church. Do not fight to expel the darkness from the chamber of your soul. Open a tiny aperture for light to enter, and the darkness will disappear.[10]

This image of the light dispelling darkness is the perfect metaphor for Elder Porphyrios's philosophy: We must fill ourselves with love for Christ, turning our attention away from temptation

---

9   Porphyrios, 54.
10   Porphyrios, 136.

and evil and looking only toward Him. This applies equally to concerns for the salvation of others: If we are concerned that our children, our spouse, or any person does not love God, rather than engaging in a battle or lecturing, we should simply turn our heart to Christ and pour out prayers. We must trust that God is the One who can transform all hearts—our own and those around us.

The Polyclinic

For many years, Elder Porphyrios had dreamt about how wonderful it would be to serve not just the spiritually unwell, but also those who struggled with physical infirmity. He thought of saints who served leper colonies and hoped that perhaps he would someday be granted such a ministry. Then in 1940, just as Greece entered World War II, Elder Porphyrios was sent to Athens, where he would serve for thirty-three years as priest of the Church of Saint Gerasimos in the Athens Polyclinic. He celebrated the services in the chapel, serving the people of the neighborhood, and also served as chaplain and spiritual father to the hospital patients and staff. He described the years as blissful precisely because he was "unknown and inconspicuous," "uneducated, insignificant and poor."[11]

Of course, people continued to come from all around to offer their confessions, but he also had time to sit with those who suffered from physical ailments and to pray in the chapel. He found true joy in the Polyclinic, saying, "I loved everyone. I felt pained for everyone, and everything moved me."[12] Through the grace of God, he saw the beauty in the work of the nurses, in the mothers nursing infants. He rejoiced in the faces he saw and in the

---

11 Porphyrios, 53.
12 Porphyrios, 56.

compassionate work they were doing. He looked around this busy Athens hospital and saw myrrhbearers everywhere, flitting about like angels.

The hospital was busy, and its neighborhood was busier: It was located in Omonia Square, one of the oldest shopping districts in the city, populated by a combination of bohemian intellectuals and anarchists, prostitutes, pickpockets, and other assorted criminals. Though he was still in Greece, Elder Porphyrios could not have been further from Mount Athos; this neighborhood was, in many ways, its opposite.

In Omonia Square, Elder Porphyrios served people from all walks of life. One year, on Theophany, he was going house to house through the neighborhood to offer blessings. He knocked on a door and realized with a start that it was a house of ill repute. He called the women forward:

> They all kissed the cross. They were all immaculately turned out with their coloured skirts and so on. And I said to them, "Blessings on you all, my children. God loves all of us. He is very good and *sends rain on the righteous and the unrighteous*. He is the Father of us all and is concerned for each one of us. Only we too must try to come to know Him and to love Him and to become good. Love Him and you'll see how happy you'll be."[13]

He greeted the young women joyfully and was honored to have blessed their home. When he looked at them, he didn't see their sins—and, indeed, he often pointed out that no one's sins are just their own; their parents and their history have great impact on their actions. Elder Porphyrios looked with the merciful eyes of Christ and saw young women made in His image, doing their best

---

13   Porphyrios, 65.

to please others by dressing beautifully. He saw that they could turn to Christ and banish this darkness from their lives, and he greeted them as if they had already done so.

On his first attempt to serve a Divine Liturgy in the Church of Saint Gerasimos, the peace was disrupted by the loud blaring of music from a nearby record store. Father was utterly disturbed by it and barely made it through the service. He asked the shop-keeper to keep the music down during Liturgy, but the man rudely refused. It was overwhelming: the noise of the street, the horns, and now this loud music. How was a monk to pray? He turned to God and fasted for three days, praying in complete silence in hope that God would reveal something simple that would tell him what to do next.

And the answer came: A boy left his schoolbook in the chapel, and Elder Porphyrios opened it. He read about the ripple effect made by stones thrown into peaceful waters. Suddenly, he knew: "The small ripples from the singing outside the church can be outflanked by the prayers of great spiritual intensity that are being said inside the church."[14] The shopkeeper could make small ripples, but the prayers of the church would be enormous rip-ples that simply overcame the others. His understanding of how grace radiates from people—as when he received the overflowing grace of Old Dimas—took on a more specific, material metaphor: Like ripples or radio waves, our prayers radiate divine energies that flow through us and impact others, transforming the world around us.[15]

---

14 Porphyrios, 57.
15 One of his most famous and beloved statements is, "You can become a saint anywhere—even in Omonia Square!"

The Elder's Wisdom

Many of Elder Porphyrios's teachings revolved around this image of radiating ripples, but they began with the love of our neighbor:

> Love toward one's brother cultivates love towards God. We are happy when we secretly love all people. Then we will feel that everyone loves us. No one can attain to God unless he first passes through his fellow men.[16]

This was his joy in the Polyclinic and throughout his life: He quietly loved everyone, as part and parcel of his love for God: "Love for God and for our neighbor; they go together and cannot be divorced."[17] We must love our fellow man if we hope to love God—there is no other path. He exhorted people,

> Let us scatter our love selflessly to all, without regards to the way they act toward us. When the grace of God enters us, we will not be concerned about whether they love us or not or whether they speak to us politely or not. We will feel the need to love all people.[18]

By radiating love toward absolutely everyone regardless of their behavior or response, we will attract God's grace—assuming, of course, that we also love God:

> The secret is our prayer and our devotion to God so that His grace may act. We, with our love, with our fervent desire for

---

16 Porphyrios, 180.
17 Porphyrios, 186.
18 Porphyrios, 182.

the love of God, will attract grace so that it washes over those around us and awakens them to divine love. Or rather God will send His love and will rouse them all. What we are unable to do, His grace will achieve. With our prayers we will make all worthy of God's love.[19]

When we are generous with our love, "scattering" it to everyone, we will find that we are more able to love God. There is an amplifying effect: Our love for each other and for God builds, and His grace enters in, and the love multiplies and radiates. Our efforts are only part of the story, for God does the rest.

Elder Porphyrios would spend his "retirement" building a monastery, and when finally he knew that his end was very near, he was able to fulfill his dearest wish: to return to the Holy Mountain, to die in peace in the hut of Saint George at Kavsokalyvia, where he had been tonsured a monk seventy years before. His last words were those of Christ's prayer, "that they all may be one" (John 17:21), for he understood that heaven is this unity: "This is the greatest mystery of our Church: that we all become one in God. If we do this we become His own. There is nothing better than this unity. This is the Orthodox faith. This is Paradise."[20]

Heaven is the union of all people with God as we enter into loving, mystical communion with Him and with all of humanity. Saint Porphyrios's great love of all people and his profound love of God were one and the same thing—inseparable, and forever building on one another. Saint Porphyrios was both a myrrhbearer himself, and one who taught myrrhbearing; he offered healing to many souls and showed each of them that love of God and others is the truest path to heaven.

---

19   Porphyrios, 185.
20   Porphyrios, 180.

FOR REFLECTION

- As a young man, St. Porphyrios knew what he wanted in life—to live on the Holy Mountain forever—but God granted him a completely different path. How did he make peace with this? How can we find peace when our paths lead us in unexpected directions?

- Saint Porphyrios found that harsh scoldings and penances drove people away from God, whereas positive measures like reading the Scriptures brought them closer. Do you suppose this was related to the age in which he lived? Were people in the twentieth century less able to stay faithful through hard penances than people in the centuries before? Why or why not?

- It is inspiring to think of loving all people, regardless of how they treat us. What are the obstacles to fulfilling this? How can we overcome them?

MOTHER GAVRILIA

Avrilia Papayanni was born in Constantinople in 1897, but she is known for having called many places home: Switzerland, Greece, England, India, Palestine, East Africa, and America.[1] A late bloomer, Avrilia was in her fifties when she began to really pursue those ministries for which we remember her. It is amazing—and perhaps inspiring to those of us on the other side of fifty—to think of what she accomplished in the second half of her life by trusting completely in God.

The First Fifty Years

A sociable, energetic, and intelligent girl, Avrilia loved her family—especially her mother—and had a happy childhood in Constantinople. Chatty and curious, she loved to tell stories about her adventures and to stare at maps, dreaming of the travels that awaited her. After high school, she took her first great adventure, moving to Switzerland to study at the School of Agriculture in Estavayer-le-Lac. She majored in botany because she had always loved plants, and until the end of her life she "talked" with them, as if she could see their response every time.

---

1 Biographical information is based on the book, *The Ascetic of Love*, by Nun Gavrilia, trans. Helen Anthony (Eptalofos SA, 1999).

In 1923, her family was part of the compulsory population exchange in which one million Greek Orthodox Christians were sent to Greece and five hundred thousand Muslims were sent to the Ottoman Empire. Avrilia joined her family in Thessaloniki and was the second woman ever admitted to Aristotle University, where she earned another degree, this time in philosophy.

When she finished school, Avrilia decided to move to England, trusting God to provide for her. She truly left it all in His hands, for she knew no one there, she had no visa, and she had only a single one-pound note in her pocket. She wasn't worried. She trusted that He would provide, and He did. Against all odds, she immediately received a visa and found a live-in situation as a governess. The whole time she was there, she never opened a bank account; instead, she would give away her money as soon as she received it.

At one point during her time in England, Avrilia served as a live-in caretaker for a woman named Miss Bright. Ever the talkative young woman, Avrilia would chatter about her life. But she observed that Miss Bright was not like Avrilia's friends, who would ask questions and offer opinions. Miss Bright was silent. She would simply keep looking at her book as she listened, and she never interrupted. Avrilia learned the value of that silence—of the ability to listen quietly, allowing the other person to continue talking as long as they needed. She began to apply that art in her own life.

One day, she happened to be walking down the street and saw a sign that said, "Chiropodist."[2] It captured her attention, so she walked into the office to learn what it meant. As she listened, she immediately felt called to it. Throughout the Second World War, Avrilia stayed in England, studying chiropody and general medicine, fascinated by the topic and by the opportunities that it would afford her to serve and heal people. In 1946 she became a doctor.

---

2   Chiropody is known in the US as podiatry, the medical treatment of feet.

This certificate was a major landmark in her life.

> Now she was independent. She had a profession that was to take her all over the world, beyond boundaries, without any worry, without any money. . . .
>
> Now spiritual horizons were opening up before her. It was the beginning of her daily contact with pain and, at the same time, of her ministry to the human soul. Ailing feet were only the pretense, the occasion. For how many people was this blessed Certificate the cause to open the eyes of their soul?[3]

As a doctor, Avrilia had a portable profession: She could practice medicine anywhere. Chiropody also gave her access to people who were in pain and seeking relief. She had found a place in people's lives where she could effect healing of soul and body.

Avrilia headed back to Greece, setting up a thriving medical practice in Athens. Her friend, Helen Virvou, wrote:

> She was working very hard, for she not only treated but also listened to people who confided to her their troubles, their worries, their misfortunes. She had become everyone's "confidant" offering to all her counsel and advice. . . . You see, even then she inspired confidence and cured the soul as well as the body. . . . I recall that she was earning 500–600 drachmas a day. By evening she had no money! . . . She had paid the rent for a blind man, had bought a suit for someone out of work. [4]

Our Lord once washed the feet of His disciples, and His servant Avrilia followed His example, humbly treating feet. As Avrilia

---

3   Gavrilia, 28–9.
4   Gavrilia, 28.

worked, she prayed the Jesus Prayer silently, and her patients poured their hearts out to her. Her myrrhbearing ministry combined physiotherapy (known as "physical therapy" in the US) and spiritual counseling. Famously, whenever she was asked why podiatry, she would reply, "Through the feet to the heart!"[5]

Avrilia offered guidance, healing, and money to anyone in need. While her skill as a doctor was unquestioned, it seems that her prayers and her loving nature effected much of the relief she provided. She did not charge anyone who could not afford her skills, and when she did make money, she gave it away as quickly as she could. If money was left over, she bought extra groceries and then left them hanging on her door when she went out so that a passerby in need would find it. She had an instinct for taking care of people, and she did so creatively and joyfully.

Turning Point

Avrilia adored her mother, and when she died in 1954, Avrilia was heartbroken. She spent that night on her knees in prayer, and throughout the night she was immersed in God's uncreated light. The experience transformed her, and she completely changed her life. She gave up her medical practice and determined to go to the place God seemed to be calling her: India.

Avrilia did not make travel arrangements or aim for a specific location in India—she just showed up and let God direct her path. At first she landed at an ashram, where she was given the job of tending to and treating the pilgrims who passed through. The first assignment was to prepare the body of an infant who had died in his mother's arms. As she cleaned and dressed him, she was deeply moved by his death. Heartbroken, tears flowed as she prayed, and

---

5   Gavrilia, 32–3.

the leader of the ashram, Sivananda, said, "Just think! A stranger has come from the end of the world to cry over this baby!"[6]

Avrilia loved much about life at the ashram, for she said, "If you have love for all the world, the whole world is beautiful."[7] She saw the good in everyone but also struggled with many things about the ashram—in particular the way the guru was celebrated as a god. At the same time, she was a Christian woman in India who had no intention of becoming Hindu—which had quite an impact on the Christian seekers who had come to India to find an exotic new religion. Many of them encountered Avrilia and found that they had traveled all the way across the world just to find themselves returning to Christ all over again.

Soon, she moved to a new location in India, AnandWan, the community of lepers established by the well-known Baba Amte. He and his family were not Christian, but they "served Him in the person of the Leper",[8] they were filled with love and gave up all their possessions, dedicating their lives to service. Avrilia described the ministry in a letter:

> AnandWan is not just a Hospital for Lepers. Here the sick are cured not only from the disease of the body but also from the equally grave affliction of the soul that accompanies this terrible sickness; the feeling of utter loneliness which is the outcome of social rejection and leads, in turn, to despair.[9]

Baba Amte's ministry was a good fit for Avrilia, and she was very inspired by her time with him. She truly came to see that we encounter Christ in the other when we serve the other, just as He

---

6   Gavrilia, 50.
7   Gavrilia, 340.
8   Gavrilia, 56.
9   Gavrilia, 59.

promised: "Assuredly, I say to you, inasmuch as you did it to one of the least of these My brethren, you did it to Me" (Matt. 25:40). As Avrilia would write in another letter, "The strange thing is that while Man often looks for Divine Inspiration in old and ruined Temples, he fails to find it in human ruins. . . . What a pity!"[10]

After four years serving in various places throughout India, Avrilia chose to spend the next year in a different way: She went to the Himalayas and spent her time in silent prayer. "She lived in Hesychia, her beloved Quietness, awaiting the Will of God, without worry or care."[11] She loved the silence but also yearned for the company of other Christians. Soon enough, local people realized that there was a very kind doctor among them, and her days became busier as patients poured in. This would no longer be a place for silence and prayer. Slowly, Avrilia began to discern what her next step would be: God was calling her to become a monastic. It was time to leave India.

In 1959 Avrilia found her way to Bethany in Palestine and the Monastery of Mary and Martha, where she was tonsured a nun and given the name Gavrilia. For three years she lived in the monastery, peacefully working on the premises and treating the occasional patient. For the rest of her life, she would travel to give talks in various countries and would live at a few different monasteries. She would say, "Any place may become a place of Resurrection, if the Humility of Christ becomes the way of our life."[12] Indeed, Mother Gavrilia's life was rooted in the humility of Christ and, therefore, in total surrender to His Providence. In all her travels and throughout her life, she did not acquire money or possessions; she abandoned herself to God and trusted Him to get her where she needed to be.

---

10 Gavrilia, 56.
11 Gavrilia, 68.
12 Gavrilia, 340.

Mother Gavrilia was a great spiritual mother to many people. Her teachings are profoundly inspiring, and like St. Porphyrios, she taught myrrhbearing as the surest path to God. She spoke of how, when we love another person, we find God within them— that is, we find Him in the Other. She taught that it is possible to so identify with the hopes, needs, and pains of another person that our own needs and concerns recede; we die to ourselves, which she likened to no longer existing:[13]

> To reach the state of non-existence, love and love and love until you identify yourself completely with the Other One, whoever this may be at the time. Then, at the end of the day, you may ask yourself: Is there anything I want? No. Is there anything I wish? No. Is there anything I lack? No. . . . So, that's it![14]

This is the natural extension of Christ's Great Commandment: When we love God with everything we have, and we love our neighbor as ourselves, we begin to approach theosis. Sister Gavrilia taught that it is through the love of others that we come to the love of God, the greatest Other One. The more we love and serve other people—that is, the more we bear myrrh—the more we empty ourselves and cease to exist as separate individuals. We die to ourselves, crucified with Christ, and find that we are transformed, born into life more abundant than we could have imagined. In that abundance, there is nothing we wish for, nothing we lack.

---

13 Perhaps because of her years in India, Mother Gavrilia often expressed her theology in terms that are not standard (or even correct) in Orthodox thinking. *Annihilation* is a good example of this: Language that is more Orthodox would avoid such a term, instead expressing her idea as emptying the self or dying to the self, moving from our existence as individuals to a higher level of ecclesial being.

14 Gavrilia, 341.

FOR REFLECTION

- Saint Gavrilia found that chiropody and, later, physiotherapy, were wonderful avenues for myrrhbearing service to the Lord. Did you find this surprising? In what way is your work an avenue for myrrhbearing?

- Saint Gavrilia spent many years in India, learning about loving service from people who were not themselves Christian. Can we learn about Christian life from people of other faiths?

- If we can love others so much that our own self-love recedes, we are becoming ever more like Christ. In some ways, this feels at odds with ideas of self-care, and yet it is clear that this kind of love brings great joy to those who experience it, like Saint Gavrilia. Is it possible that this way of living creates a sort of "living water" that never runs out (John 4:10)? What is the difference between this kind of sacrificial love and the kind of service that wears us down and leaves us exhausted and empty?

MARIA SKOBTSOVA
(MOTHER MARIA
OF PARIS)

Elizaveta Pilenko, known to family and friends as Liza, was born in Latvia in 1891, when it was part of the Russian Empire.[1] Her family were faithful Orthodox Christians, and she loved them very much. Her father was the mayor of a village called Anapa, and Liza would eventually follow in his footsteps. She adored her father, but when she was fourteen, tragedy struck: Liza's father died. In her lifetime she would endure many griefs, and she would come to find that turning to God in these moments brings both consolation and revelation. But at fourteen, she could not make sense of her pain. How could God allow her father to die? He couldn't—which meant that either God was not real, or He was not the loving God she believed Him to be. Liza became an atheist.

---

1   Biographical details can be found at www.oca.org/saints/lives, July 20, "Righteous Martyr Maria (Skobtsova)" and in *Pearl of Great Price: The Life of Mother Maria Skobtsova 1891–1945* by Sergei Hackel (St. Vladimir's Seminary Press, 1965).

All Talk and No Action

As she grew older, Liza moved to St. Petersburg, where she spent time in cafés talking to wild-eyed revolutionaries. It was exciting—they were going to change the world. Liza had deep sympathy for the poor and downtrodden, and she was eager to be part of a movement that was finally going to do something to help them. At age 19, Liza married one of these revolutionaries, and before long the couple had a daughter, Gaiana. But time passed, and the revolutionaries continued to sit and talk about radical ideas and about all the big changes they were going to make. Liza grew restless. There was so much talk, but no action. None of these people were doing anything to help the people. They were just talking.

Liza began to think of Jesus' teachings about mercy and compassion for the least of our brothers. As time passed, she found herself drawn back toward the Church. She began to pray again and read the Gospels and the lives of saints. She returned to the Faith, making peace with God and deciding that what the people of her country really needed was not a revolution, but Jesus Christ. Liza and her husband divorced, and she was accepted as the very first female student at the Theological Academy of the Alexander Nevsky Monastery in St. Petersburg. She soon would marry again, this time to a man named Daniel Skobtsova. Due to the political issues there, including a civil war, they moved their family out of Russia.

They moved from place to place, and along the way Liza gave birth to two more children: her son, Yura, and her daughter, Anastasia (Nastia). The family settled in Paris, among a sizable Russian community taking refuge from the communist regime. Liza made dolls and painted silk scarves to help provide for her family, and soon she began to help struggling Russian refugees.

The Two-Sided Coin of Grief

In the winter of 1926, the entire family suffered from influenza. It seemed that Nastia suffered its aftereffects for some time, until it became clear that something else was wrong. She was eventually diagnosed with tuberculous meningitis, and Liza sat at her side for two months in a hospital as her condition slowly deteriorated. Nastia's death changed everything for Liza. In her own words, she wrote:

> Into the grave's dark maw are plunged all hopes, plans, habits, calculations and, above all, meaning, the whole meaning of life. In the face of this, everything needs to be re-examined or rejected, to be measured against falsehood and corruption.
>
> People call this a visitation of the Lord. A visitation which brings what? Grief? No, more than grief: for he suddenly reveals the true nature of things, and on the one hand we perceive the dead remains of one who was alive, . . . the mortality of all creation, while on the other hand we simultaneously perceive the life-giving, fiery, all-penetrating and all-consuming Comforter, the Spirit.[2]

This great grief made Liza reassess everything in her life. The pain and desolation of death simultaneously revealed the glorious Comforter, the Holy Spirit. She began to yearn to live a more real, purer Christian life, and she threw herself into her work with Russian refugees. As is often the case when children die, her marriage suffered. The couple agreed to live apart, so Daniel and Yura moved out.

---

2   Hackel, 5.

Liza traveled around France for a group called the Russian Christian Student Movement in Exile, speaking to groups of Russians in various towns and villages. On her visits she came into contact with despairing Russians. Among these refugee communities, alcoholism ran rampant, suicide rates were high, and the people were miserable. As Liza described it:

> I would find myself transformed from an official lecturer into a confessor. As soon as I came to know the people we would embark on frank conversations about émigré life or else about the past. And my companions—no doubt sensing me to be a sympathetic listener—would try to find a spare minute afterwards to talk to me alone. A queue would form by the door as if outside a confessional. There would be people wanting to pour out their hearts, to tell of some terrible grief which had burdened them for years, of pangs of conscience which gave them no peace. In such slums it is no use speaking of faith in God, of Christ or of the Church. What is needed here is not religious preaching, but the simplest thing of all: compassion.[3]

Liza understood that sometimes people need edification, sometimes they need food or shelter, and sometimes they just need to be heard and understood. The people she met needed to unburden themselves, and in her generosity, Liza sat and listened for hours, responding only with compassion. In her encounters with refugees, Liza was a true myrrhbearer.

Liza was struck by the fact that she could never do enough for the people she encountered, and as she continued her journeys, she developed a "code of practice"—a method with which she would approach service:

---

3   Hackel, 11.

If someone turns with his spiritual world to the spiritual world of another person, he encounters an awesome and inspiring mystery. . . . He comes into contact with the true image of God in man, with the very icon of God incarnate in the world, with a reflection of the mystery of God's incarnation and divine manhood. And he needs to accept this awesome revelation of God unconditionally, to venerate the image of God in his brother. Only when he senses, perceives and understands it will yet another mystery be related to him—one that will demand his most dedicated efforts.[4]

Liza came to understand that when we encounter one another, we are encountering God; God reveals himself to us in other people. She embraced radical acceptance—the offer of unconditional love for the other. What's more, she was increasingly confident that the care we offer must be holistic—it must take into account the physical, the spiritual, and the psychological:

Man ought to treat the body of his fellow human being with more care than he treats his own. Christian love teaches us to give our fellows material as well as spiritual gifts. We should give them our last shirt and our last piece of bread. Personal almsgiving and the most wide-ranging social work are both equally justified and needed.[5]

Liza understood both the significance and the complexity of myrrhbearing: She saw that it was not an either/or situation, in which we might choose to provide spiritual advice instead of food or social services; instead, she found that serving must be both/

---

4   Hackel, 13.
5   Hackel, 14.

and. We are called to do everything we can for our brothers and sisters, just as God blesses us abundantly in a variety of ways.

A Monastic in the World

Liza wanted to serve God more intently, and in 1932, she was tonsured a nun. She took the name Maria, with the understanding that she would found a new convent—the first Russian monastery in exile in France. At one point, she was able to visit a traditional Russian monastery in Riga, and she was not impressed, dismissing them as "bourgeois" and saying, "No one [there] is aware that the world is on fire. There is no concern for the fate of the world."[6]

Metropolitan Evlogii encouraged her to develop a new kind of "monasticism in the world": Rather than retreat to a monastery, she could be a nun in the city, serving people in need. As Maria would later say, "The more we go out into the world, the more we give ourselves to the world, the less we are of the world. For the worldly do not give the world an offering of themselves."[7]

Just as traditional monasticism withdrew from the world, Maria saw that by giving themselves selflessly *to* the world, she and the nuns who served with her would distinguish themselves *from* the selfish world. Ultimately, either way, the monastic still would be distanced from the world.

And so Mother Maria began her ministry in Paris. She began with one house, where she welcomed Russian refugees, providing food and other assistance. An upstairs room became the chapel, and Mother Maria painted the iconostasis. People came to help her, and the need was so great that before long she set up in an additional, larger home. She and her helpers served dinner to as

---

6 Hackel, 22–3.
7 Hackel, 27.

many as 120 people every night. Sometimes they would turn the dining room into a hall where Orthodox speakers would come to teach about the Faith. At this new house, the stables were made into a chapel, and again Mother Maria helped with the icons. Some of her icons were embroidered; others were painted. Mother Maria rented additional buildings for needy families to live in, started a hospital, began schools, and was always looking for Russian refugees to help. She went to the mental hospitals and found that Russians who could not speak French had been misunderstood and committed, so she worked to have them released then took them in.

Maria was a bit unruly for a nun. She grew frustrated with those who suggested that her ministry needed to be more structured in terms of religious services and observations. For instance, there were Sundays when Mother Maria was busily building an icon screen or cooking a meal, and she did not attend Liturgy. She was exasperated when others would suggest a more measured approach to meeting the needs of the people entrusted to her, saying, for instance, "Piety, piety, but where is the love that removes mountains? The further I go, the more I accept that it alone is the measure of things. All the rest is more or less necessary external discipline."[8]

Perhaps her most famous statement is:

The way to God lies through love of people. At the Last Judgment I shall not be asked whether I was successful in my ascetic exercises, nor how many bows and prostrations I made. Instead I shall be asked did I feed the hungry, clothe the naked, visit the sick and the prisoners. That is all I shall be asked. About every poor, hungry and imprisoned person the Savior says "I": "I was hungry and thirsty, I was sick and in prison." To think that he

---

8   Hackel, 42.

puts an equal sign between himself and anyone in need. . . . I always knew it, but now it has somehow penetrated to my sinews. It fills me with awe.[9]

Mother Maria was confident that God wanted her working, and she was far less concerned with her church attendance.

Nazi Occupation

When World War II began and the Nazis occupied Paris, Mother Maria made every effort to save as many Jewish people as she could. She worked with her priest, Fr. Dimitri, to help: They filled out false baptismal certificates so that Jews could pretend to be Christian to avoid the concentration camps. Mother Maria, her son Yura, and Fr. Dimitri planned escape routes for Jewish people and assisted them on their journey to safety.

In 1942 the Nazis would gather up Jews and bring them to the Velodrome, or the Winter Stadium, which they were using as a holding place until they could be taken to Nazi death camps. Mother Maria found a way in. Thousands of Jewish people were there, days away from entering concentration camps, and Mother Maria could make only a small dent. She made an arrangement with some of Paris's trash haulers, and they helped her smuggle children out of the Velodrome inside trash cans. They drove the children in garbage trucks to Mother Maria's house, where she would arrange for their escape from Paris. The house was soon filled with Jewish people, and she and her helpers worked feverishly to save them from certain death.

In 1943 Mother Maria was caught. The Nazis arrested her, along with Fr. Dimitri and Yura, for helping the Jews. The men were

---

9   Hackel, 29.

sent to the Dora concentration camp, and she was sent to Ravens-bruck. Even while she was a prisoner in that camp, Mother Maria's faith in God never wavered. She grew unrecognizable, emaciated and prematurely aged. There are several versions of the story of her passing, but the most probable seems to be the most peaceful and characteristically generous: On Great and Holy Friday, April 30, 1945, as Russian soldiers advanced and Germany was on the verge of surrender, Mother Maria was with a group of anxious women who were being transported to a gas chamber. She stood among them, comforting them, and as the group moved along, she simply moved along with them. She seems to have entered the transport with them, to calm them and to be company on this terrible jour-ney, despite the death sentence she was implicitly accepting. On the next day, Holy Saturday, as the war ended and the Red Cross arrived to help those in the camps, and as the first three hundred prisoners were released from her camp, Mother Maria died in the gas chamber.

A true myrrhbearer, Mother Maria was unapologetic and uncompromising. She did not just feed, clothe, visit, and help the others in her care; she found in every person an icon of God, and she engaged in connection with the divine with every encoun-ter. She poured herself fearlessly into her work with a strength of conviction that is truly rare. When the Nazis came to destroy the Jewish population of France, Mother Maria's response was charac-teristically bold, as she spared no effort to save people and wasted no energy on protecting herself. Even months in concentration camps could not break her spirit or her profound love, and she would not stop serving and caring for others, even until the last terrible moment.

FOR REFLECTION

- Not all saints are gentle and quiet. Saint Maria of Paris was rough around the edges, outspoken, and tough. How did she turn her particular personality traits to service for God?

- Do you recognize characteristics in your own personality that feel "unsaintly"? Is there a way to put them to use for God?

- Saint Maria of Paris saw that Christ identified with the hungering prisoner, and she did so as well—to the point of entering the gas chamber before she was officially called to it. What does it take to quell the fear of death and enter into death in order to calm fellow prisoners?

AFTERWORD

There is a folk story—not a true story, of course, but a fun one—that St. Maria Skobstova is said to have enjoyed very much: St. Nicholas and St. John Cassian were in heaven, and they wanted to check on things back on earth. As soon as they arrived, they came across a peasant whose cart had slipped into a muddy ditch. He asked for help, and St. John Cassian apologetically explained that he would be returning to heaven soon and had to keep his heavenly white garment spotlessly clean. Saint Nicholas did not answer at all, for he was already knee deep in mud, using all of his strength to free the man's cart. When they returned to heaven and explained the state of their garments, God looked at both of His saints, and His love flowed over them.

"John Cassian, my beloved," God said, "you have indeed kept your heart in heaven, and your hands are clean of all things of the earth. And the heart of my beloved Nicholas is turned toward the people, however earthly their cares might be, and his hands are quick to help them when they call on him. And this," he said, "is why Nicholas, my beloved, has feast days in both summer and winter and why he's honored every Thursday besides. And this is why you, my beloved John Cassian, have but one feast day every four years" (February 29).

As silly as this story is, it hinges on the idea that there are two kinds of holiness: a purity that is otherworldly and untouchable, and a holiness marked by co-suffering and practicality. Myrrh-bearers rarely keep their hands clean. Whether it's Tobit sleeping in the courtyard, unclean from burying the unfortunate dead, or Mother Maria missing Liturgy because she is receiving a new refugee at the house, myrrhbearers tend to be focused on *doing the work* and are willing to enter into the struggle, the suffering, and the messiness of those they serve.

In this book we have considered many ways to live out the calling of the myrrhbearer. We have seen the traditional, funeral myrrhbearing of those who accompanied Christ to His Tomb, who—like Tobit—were guided by a love too stubborn to fail. We have reflected on St. Basil's ideal Christian space, where everyone was welcomed and offered medical treatment and nourishment, prayer and hugs, and the opportunity to give and receive love in community.

From St. John the Merciful we have learned about a mindset that encourages mercy—reminding ourselves that anyone could be our Lord in disguise, identifying with the one in need, and remembering that death is imminent. From Ss. Cosmas and Damian, we have been given an example of the importance of giving without hope of remuneration, but we have also discovered a cautionary tale about the danger of holding too tightly to our rule—of committing fratricide in the name of brotherly love.

Righteous Joseph's most obvious myrrhbearing service is saving the known world from famine; yet perhaps his most inspiring myrrhbearing act is his ability to forgive, which comes from an unwavering trust in God's Providence. Saint Stylianos in his humble service; St. John Maximovitch, the Barefoot Bishop, in his tireless devotion to his flock; and St. Nicholas, whose left hand never knew what his right hand was doing, all gave of themselves generously, and their lives became rivers of healing myrrh. Both

St. Nicholas and St. Herman show us that myrrhbearers defend those who are unfairly accused. We have considered how St. Herman managed to live as an ascetic in the wilderness while also serving as the beating heart of a community that benefited from his protection and guidance.

From St. Olga we have learned something about emptying ourselves in the most mundane and wonderful service, becoming a mother to all and a healing presence to women who have suffered abuse. Bishop Basil Rodzianko shows us how to communicate with God by saying yes to the human beings He created, and St. Porphyrios built upon that foundation of joyful obedience, demonstrating how we might radiate Christ and His grace to the people around us. Saint Gavrilia shows us that we can grow to identify with the Other, just as Christ identifies with the least of these. And St. Maria of Paris teaches us to venerate the image of God in our brother—to come into contact with the divine by entering into communion with one another.

We have seen that the greatest myrrhbearers have lived ascetic, prayerful lives, deep in the Scriptures and the lives of the saints, and they have encountered God when they've entered into the suffering of others. As St. John the Evangelist says, "No one has seen God at any time. If we love one another, God abides in us, and his love has been perfected in us" (1 John 4:12). When we enter into communion with one another, serving humbly and in selfless love, we find that God is there, inside every one of us. Our communion with Him and our communion with mankind miraculously blend together.

This is a transformation: God is love, and His love is made complete in us. This is how we become ecclesial beings, truly a part of the Body of Christ. We become partakers in His love, and through His grace we are transformed, as these beautiful myrrhbearers have been. Myrrhbearing is service to the Other—that is, to the other person, and also to God—and before long, it becomes an encounter with God.

It's likely that we all are doing our share of myrrhbearing—that we are serving the people we find on our path. But there's always more to do, not simply because the problem is large—for there are so many people hungering, suffering, and hurting—but because this is our opportunity. This is the surest path to theosis, to union with God. By focusing on the needs of others, we move our attention away from our own needs and comforts until they lose their sway over us. Of course, we don't simply run ourselves into the ground, for the myrrhbearer's own body counts as an important human body as well! Rather, as St. Paul advises, "he who shows mercy [should do so] with cheerfulness" (Rom. 12:8), and,

> He who sows sparingly will also reap sparingly, and he who sows bountifully will also reap bountifully. *So let* each one *give* as he purposes in his heart, not grudgingly or of necessity; for God loves a cheerful giver. And God *is* able to make all grace abound toward you, that you, always having all sufficiency in all *things,* may have an abundance for every good work. (2 Cor. 9:6–8)

This dying to ourselves must be cheerful—and we see this attitude in all the myrrhbearers we have met. At the heart of myrrhbearing we do not find misery or self-abuse, but a profoundly joyful offering to God, which He answers with ever more grace and love. This is an endless cycle of ever-increasing abundant love, in which we soon find that though we have denied ourselves everything, we want for nothing.

If we can learn the art of myrrhbearing, of becoming humble and compassionate, obedient and caretaking, we will find that life is ever more abundant. We will see our hearts become aflame with love, and we will radiate that love into the people and places around us. We can die to our personal preferences and our own will and be born into a new life of deep communion and grace. Then our hearts will sing out in joy, no matter our circumstances.

FOR REFLECTION

- How does myrrhbearing look in your life today?

- Do you radiate Christ?

- What is your next step?

POSTSCRIPT:
ONE MORE MYRRHBEARER

While researching the myrrhbearers and their lives, I came across one more myrrhbearer that I should mention: the icon. In the Orthodox Christian tradition, we venerate icons. Because Christ took on flesh and a body like ours, it is now permissible to depict Him; and because His Incarnation is so important, we honor the materiality of the icon, making what is real in heaven visible on earth as well.

We never worship icons, but we understand that they act as windows to heaven, portals that allow us to glimpse, with the eyes of our heart, "since we are surrounded by so great a cloud of witnesses" (Heb. 12:1).

And every once in a while, something beautiful happens: An icon begins to stream myrrh. It's a small miracle of no obvious consequence—it's not a resurrection or a lightning strike, and it doesn't always heal anyone or solve any problems. It's just a little bit of sweet-smelling oil to let us know that we are seen and loved.

I know a couple who were struggling to have a child. They suffered miscarriages, always turning to God in their grief and anxiety. One day, the wife found that she was pregnant again, and she wondered where she would find the strength to move through this pregnancy, always fearing the worst. As they prayed together in front of their icons, tiny droplets of myrrh began to form on the icon of Mary, the Mother of God. Her fingers grew wet with myrrh, as if she wanted to reach out to anoint this sweet couple. The husband anointed his wife with the oil, and she felt strengthened and reassured. They were not alone; the Theotokos was watching over them.

As the pregnancy progressed, at various critical junctures and during all the scariest moments, they would approach to pray, and the icon would stream myrrh again. Again and again, the wife was anointed. Throughout the pregnancy, the couple knew they were not alone; the Mother of God was comforting them—bearing myrrh for them in more than one way. They gave birth to a healthy daughter, and the icon stopped issuing myrrh. Years later, they continue to thank God for His blessings.

When an icon streams myrrh, we know that our tears have been seen, that we are not alone in our sorrows. The beautiful, intense fragrance of the myrrh—quite unlike anything one finds in this world—is a whiff of the Kingdom, a promise of the life to come.

FOR REFLECTION

- Myrrhbearing can take many forms. How do icons show us that the cloud of witnesses co-suffers with us?

- In what other ways do the saints offer company and solace?

- Have you ever been visited in this way by a saint or perhaps by a loved one who has passed away? Has their company made you feel less alone? Has it given you a small taste of the Kingdom to come?

We hope you have enjoyed and benefited from this book. Your financial support makes it possible to continue our nonprofit ministry both in print and online. Because the proceeds from our book sales only partially cover the costs of operating **Ancient Faith Publishing** and **Ancient Faith Radio**, we greatly appreciate the generosity of our readers and listeners. Donations are tax deductible and can be made at **www.ancientfaith.com**.

To view our other publications,
please visit our website:
store.ancientfaith.com

 ANCIENT FAITH RADIO

Bringing you Orthodox Christian music, readings,
prayers, teaching, and podcasts 24 hours a day since 2004 at
www.ancientfaith.com